VIEVASS.—

MARCH 2003.

freshfood**fast**

freshfoodfast

over 175 original recipes and ideas that take
only 15 minutes to prepare

quadrille

First published in 2001 by
Quadrille Publishing Limited
Alhambra House
27-31 Charing Cross Road
London WC2H OLS

The material in this volume was previously published
in *BBC Good Food* magazine.

Front cover photograph by Roger Stowell
Back cover photographs by Martin Brigdale, Ian Wallace,
Jean Cazals and Roger Stowell

ISBN 1 902757 97 1

Editor & Project Manager: **Lewis Esson**
Editorial Director: **Jane O'Shea**
Art Director: **Mary Evans**
Design Assistant: **Jim Smith**
Project Editor for the BBC: **Vicki Vrint**
Production: **Julie Hadingham**

Printed and bound in Singapore by Star Standard Industries (Pte) Ltd
Colour separations by Colourscan, Singapore

• Throughout the book recipes are for four people unless
  otherwise stated.
• Both metric and imperial quantities are given. Use either
  all metric or all imperial, as the two are not necessarily
  interchangeable.

contents

introduction 6

speedy starters, snacks & soups 10

lightning light meals & brunches 30

fast family fare 50

effortless entertaining 74

dashing desserts 98

trouble-free teatime treats 128

acknowledgements 140

index 142

introduction

You've got less than an hour to get back, prepare a family meal or something nice for friends and you have to do the shopping on the way home. Sounds familiar? Nowadays the easy answer for so many of us in these circumstances is supermarket convenience food, but that needn't be your only option – such ready-meals are also expensive and can be full of unhealthy additives. How much better to make your own dishes using simple fresh ingredients, singing with flavour... and so much better for your purse and your health.

The recipes in *Fresh Food Fast* demonstrate that by making the right choices and developing a few useful short-cuts you can put together a wide range of mouthwatering dishes for all occasions. Our simple criterion has been to include only recipes that require a preparation time of 15 minutes or less, allowing us also to feature dishes that involve the minimum of preparation followed by the long slow cooking, marinating, chilling or freezing that produces richly developed flavours and comfort food. So only a little advance planning and very little work will bring sumptuous food to the table minutes after you've been shopping, working or even relaxing.

useful equipment

Apart from one or two good sharp knives and sturdy pans (preferably with tight-fitting lids), you don't really need specialist equipment to cook fresh food fast. However these are invaluable time-savers:

Food processor
These obviously speed chopping and mixing in any situation. Try to get one with a detachable small bowl for small amounts. If you can manage to give your food processor permanent space out on a work top this not only saves time it means that you will use it more readily.

Scissors
Have a couple of good pairs of all-purpose kitchen scissors and keep them sharp. They are useful for everything from jointing poultry to snipping herbs.

Zester
A lemon zester allows you to pare off strips of peel from citrus fruit without lifting up the bitter pith underneath.

Salad spinner
A salad spinner gets leaves really dry and saves a lot of time otherwise spent patting them.

Pastry brush
A good stout pastry or paint brush is useful for applying oil to food, grill racks, ridged grilling pans, etc., but avoid nylon bristles as they do often melt on contact with hot utensils.

Wok
A wok is essential for stir-frying. Get one with a matching scoop with which to stir the food. Buy the very basic and inexpensive ones from Chinese supermarkets which may be replaced readily.

Ridged grilling pan
This heats quickly (you do have to have a gas hob) and seals and cooks steaks, chops, small whole fish etc. in minutes. It also gives you the chance to get a feeling of barbecued food quickly (and in the rain!) and also to get the decorative effect of sear marks on your cooked meats.

Frying pans
If you can, try to have one or two frying pans in different sizes to match the type and quantity of food being cooked. Non-stick frying pans are best as they facilitate healthy dry-frying. A small omelette pan is also very useful.

the prepared pantry

As with most things, the secret to being able to produce good fresh food fast, is simply being prepared. It is amazing how many dishes you can put together in a hurry, with the minimum of fuss and extra shopping, if your kitchen is well stocked. Obviously you don't need to have all of the following all of the time, but none of it will go to waste.

in the larder:

loaf of good bread
half dozen eggs
1 or 2 heads of garlic
packet of sea salt
packet of black peppercorns
4 or 5 red onions
4 or 5 lemons
3 or 4 limes
2 or 3 oranges

in the fridge:

600ml/1pt milk
225g/8oz unsalted butter
225g/8oz unsmoked streaky bacon
300ml/½pt plain runny yoghurt
300ml/½pt crème fraîche, double cream or fromage frais
large chunk of Parmesan cheese
225g/8oz Cheddar cheese
packet of ready-washed salad leaves
bunch of spring onions
2–3 red or yellow peppers
1 or 2 chilli peppers
450g/1lb tasty tomatoes
jar of good made mustard
bottle of dry white wine

on the window-sill:

fresh herbs, especially chives, flat-leaf parsley, basil, dill

in the freezer:

another loaf of good bread
another 225g/8oz unsalted butter
packet of muffins
225g/8oz leaf spinach
115g/4oz small garden peas
1 litre/1¾pt good vanilla ice-cream
1.1 litre/2pt chicken stock

in the store cupboard:

450g/1lb basmati rice
450g/1lb pasta
450g/1lb easy-cook Oriental noodles
bottle of extra-virgin olive oil
bottle of olive oil (for cooking)
bottle of sunflower oil
small bottle of dark sesame oil
bottle of red or white wine vinegar or cider vinegar
small bottle of balsamic vinegar
bottle of good-quality soy sauce
tin of English mustard powder
tin of five-spice powder
large bottle of Worcestershire sauce
large jar of good-quality mayonnaise (keep in fridge once opened)
tube or bottle of anchovy essence (keep in fridge once opened)
tube of tomato paste (keep in fridge once opened)
bottle of Tabasco sauce
packet of whole nutmegs
drum of paprika
packet of cumin seeds
packet of oregano
packet of small dried chillies
packet of dried wild mushrooms
jar of sun-dried tomatoes in oil

useful techniques

Chiffonnade
A quick way of shredding salad and herb leaves is to pile them on top of each other, roll up tightly and then snip the roll across with scissors.

Tearing
You can, of course, simply tear food like salad leaves or cooked chicken into bowls or pans. This is not only quicker than chopping but gives a better texture and keeps more of their juices.

Crumbling and flaking
Crumbling and flaking foods like cheese and cooked poultry and fish rather than chopping them can save you an amazing amount of time.

Using garlic
A quick and easy means of flavouring with garlic is to halve a clove and rub it over the bottom of a pan or bowl or even smear it directly over firm food. Otherwise crush cloves with the flat of a knife or use a garlic press.

Grilling
When grilling, remember to turn on the grill as early as possible so that it has the time to get properly heated while you are preparing the ingredients. Try to use only uniformly thin pieces of food for quick and even cooking.

Pan-grilling
The secret with pan-grilling is also to get it nice and hot before you start. Place the food carefully on it and leave undisturbed until the surface in contact is fairly well cooked. You can always test by edging up a little corner. Turn carefully and repeat with the other side. If the food being pan-grilled does not have much natural fat, then first grease the pan well with oil, preferably a vegetable oil that takes high temperatures well like groundnut.

Chopping onions: cut in half lengthwise, put half cut-side down and slice lengthwise, keeping root intact, then cut across into tiny dice.

Snipping: snip herbs like chives – even spring onions – with scissors directly into a dish or over a salad, etc., rather than chopping them on boards.

Processing: first break the food into manageable pieces, then process just long enough to get desired texture and don't over-process foods to a mush.

Deseeding tomatoes: halve the tomatoes across and then simply squeeze the seeds out over a bowl or directly into the sink.

1

When in a hurry, it's too tempting to snack on convenience food or not bother with a first course. However, there are so many exciting ways – involving little or no cooking – to produce that light bite which satisfies or sets the scene for what will then look like a very considered meal.

speedy starters, snacks & soups

roast asparagus with garlic and capers

Preparation 5 minutes Cooking 15 minutes

350g/12oz asparagus

2 tbsp olive oil

1 large garlic clove, cut into very thin slices

1 tbsp large capers in brine, rinsed and drained

juice of ½ orange

1 Preheat the oven to 200°C/400°F/Gas 6. Bring a large pan of water to the boil. Add the asparagus and boil for 2 minutes until still crisp but beginning to become tender. Drain and refresh under cold water. Pat dry on kitchen paper.

2 Pour the oil into a shallow roasting tin and roll the asparagus in it to coat. Scatter over the garlic slivers and capers and roast for 8–10 minutes, until the asparagus is tinged with brown and cooked through – test by inserting the tip of a knife into a few of the thicker spears.

3 Sprinkle with the orange juice, season and serve warm.

roast asparagus and prosciutto bundles

Preparation 5 minutes Cooking about 15 minutes

This simple seasonal starter can be prepared several hours ahead.

a little olive oil, for brushing

salt and pepper

250g/9oz asparagus

4 slices of prosciutto

fresh Parmesan shavings, to serve

for the dressing

2 tbsp walnut oil

1 tbsp olive oil

1 tbsp fresh lemon juice

1 Preheat the oven to 200°C/400°F/Gas 6 and oil a baking sheet. Bring a pan of salted water to the boil, add the asparagus and cook for 2 minutes to parboil, then drain and refresh under cold water.

2 Divide the asparagus into 4 bundles and wrap a slice of prosciutto around each bundle. Arrange on the oiled baking sheet and brush the asparagus lightly with oil. (The bundles can be prepared ahead up to this stage, covered and chilled until you are ready to cook them.)

3 Roast the bundles for 10 minutes, until the prosciutto is crisp and the asparagus lightly browned.

4 Meanwhile, make the dressing: whisk the ingredients together in a small bowl until slightly thickened, then season with salt and pepper.

5 Transfer each bundle to a warm serving plate and drizzle over the dressing. Garnish with Parmesan shavings, add a fresh sprinkling of pepper and serve warm.

prawn and mango cocktail

Preparation 10 minutes

This is a fresh take on the classic prawn cocktail. Instead of the rather ketchupy 'sauce Marie-Rose' of yesteryear, this version is topped with a lime-coriander mayonnaise.

a few crisp lettuce leaves
5cm/2 inch piece of cucumber
1 small ripe mango
200–300g/8–10oz peeled cooked
   prawns
4 tbsp mayonnaise
1 lime
generous pinch of chilli powder,
   plus more for sprinkling
1 tbsp chopped fresh coriander
   leaves
salt and pepper

1 Shred the lettuce and divide it between 4 glass serving dishes. Peel strips of skin from the cucumber skin lengthwise, then cut it in half lengthwise. Cut each half at an angle into thin slices.

2 Cut the mango in half either side of the flat stone. Pare off the skin, then cut the flesh into thin slices. Arrange the cucumber and mango slices over the lettuce, then pile the prawns on top.

3 Mix the mayonnaise with the juice of half the lime (reserving the other half), the chilli powder, coriander and salt and pepper. (You can prepare ahead up to this point.)

4 To serve: spoon the mayonnaise over the prawns and sprinkle lightly with more chilli powder. Cut the reserved lime half into 4 wedges and serve separately for squeezing over the prawn cocktail.

melon with mint, ginger and orange

Preparation 10 minutes

Melon was once a treat. We're blasé about it now, but a simply dressed ripe melon is one of nature's wonders. This dish can be made up to 6 hours ahead and chilled. Remove it from the fridge about 10 minutes before serving.

1 ripe melon, such as a Cantaloupe
   or Charentais, peeled, deseeded
   and cut into thin slices
1cm/½inch piece of root ginger,
   peeled and cut into thin strips
grated zest of ½ orange
juice of 1 large orange
handful of shredded mint leaves

1 Arrange the melon slices on plates.

2 Mix the ginger, orange zest and juice; drizzle this over the melon, then sprinkle over the mint.

Variation
Cut the orange rind into strips instead of grating it, if you prefer.

fried prawns with chilli and lime leaf

Serves 6

Preparation 10 minutes Cooking about 2 minutes

Thai meals aim to include different textures and tastes, so a fried dish is often included, whether it is something dipped in a crispy batter and fried, or a stir-fry, as in this prawn dish. Jars of Thai red curry paste and bottles of Thai fish sauce are now readily available from better supermarkets, delis and food stores.

3 tbsp oil
3 garlic cloves, finely chopped
2 tbsp Thai red curry paste
3 tbsp stock or water
400g/14oz large raw prawns,
   shelled and deveined
2 tbsp Thai fish sauce (nam pla)
1½ tbsp caster sugar
1½ tbsp fresh lemon juice
3 lime leaves, finely shredded

1 In a wok or frying pan, heat the oil and fry the garlic until golden. Stir in the red curry paste and cook together for a few seconds. Add the stock or water and mix thoroughly.

2 Tip in the prawns and cook for a few seconds over a very high heat, until the prawns are evenly pink.

3 Stirring quickly after each addition, add the fish sauce, sugar, lemon juice and lime leaves in that order.

4 Stir thoroughly for 2–3 seconds and serve.

kung pao prawns

Serves 6

Preparation 10 minutes Cooking 5 minutes

To bring out their flavour, dry-roast the peanuts in a pan over a medium heat. Roasted salted peanuts are far too salty. Remember to allow 15 minutes for standing.

30 large shelled raw prawns
1 tsp cornflour
2 tbsp groundnut oil
25g/1oz raw peanuts in their skins,
   roasted, then the skins rubbed off
1 small red chilli, deseeded and
   thinly sliced
2 spring onions, cut into slivers

for the sauce
1 tsp Sichuan peppercorns
3 tbsp rice vinegar
2 tbsp hoisin sauce
1 tbsp light soy sauce
½ tsp crushed dried red chillies
1 tsp dark sesame oil

1 Cut into each prawn along the top side (not all the way through) and pull out the black vein. Sprinkle the prawns with cornflour, then rub it over to coat them. Leave to stand for 15 minutes.

2 Make the sauce: put the peppercorns in a small frying pan over a medium heat. Cook, shaking the pan frequently, for 2–3 minutes, until the peppercorns darken slightly and smell toasted. Grind coarsely using a pestle and mortar. Stir in the rice vinegar, hoisin and soy sauces and the dried chillies.

3 Heat a wok over a high heat until very hot. Pour in the oil, swirling to coat the sides. Add the prawns and stir-fry until they turn pink, about 1½ minutes.

4 Stir in the sauce with the sesame oil and heat through. Toss in the peanuts and serve, sprinkled with the sliced chilli and spring onion.

mixed leaves with feta and griddled peaches

Preparation 5 minutes Cooking 5 minutes

oil, for greasing
juice of 1 lime
4 ripe peaches, each cut into wedges
200g/7oz bag of mixed salad leaves
300g/10½oz jar of marinated feta
  cheese in oil
1 red onion, sliced
2 tbsp chopped fresh mint
salt and pepper

1 Heat a lightly greased griddle pan until just smoking. Squeeze the lime juice over the peaches and place them on the griddle pan. Cook them for 2–3 minutes, turning, until pleasantly charred.

2 In a large salad bowl, mix together the salad leaves, the feta cut into cubes, 2 tablespoons of the oil from the feta, the red onion and the chopped mint. Season well.

3 Divide the mixture between 4 plates and top with the charred peaches. Sprinkle over some black pepper and serve.

fig and goats' cheese salad

Preparation 5 minutes

8 slices of prosciutto
4 ripe figs, quartered
bag of salad leaves
100g/4oz soft goats' cheese,
  crumbled

for the dressing
5 tbsp olive oil
2 tbsp red wine vinegar
1 tbsp honey
1 tsp fresh thyme leaves
salt and pepper

1 First make the dressing: mix together the ingredients and season.

2 Put 2 prosciutto slices and a quartered fig on each plate. Top with the salad leaves, then crumble over the cheese.

3 Drizzle over the dressing and serve.

gnocchi with broad beans and mushrooms

Preparation 5 minutes Cooking 10 minutes

Potato gnocchi are a useful energy-giving carbohydrate base for a dish, and if bought vacuum-packed they make a great fridge or freezer standby. Mascarpone cheese and lemon juice combine to make a fresh-tasting sauce. Add a handful of chopped parsley if you don't have tarragon.

350g/12oz potato gnocchi

2 tbsp olive oil

250g/9oz small-cup mushrooms, halved

2 garlic cloves, crushed

200g/7oz frozen baby broad beans

3 tbsp chopped fresh tarragon

250g/9oz mascarpone cheese

1 tbsp lemon juice

salt and pepper

Parmesan shavings and pared lemon zest, to garnish

salad leaves, to serve (optional)

1 Cook the gnocchi according to the packet instructions. Drain and set aside.

2 Heat the oil in a frying pan, add the mushrooms and fry quickly over a high heat until browned. Lift out with a slotted spoon and add to the gnocchi.

3 Wipe out the pan, then add the garlic, beans, tarragon and mascarpone. Heat gently, stirring, until the mascarpone has melted. Add the lemon juice, mushrooms and gnocchi. Heat through for 1 minute, then season to taste.

4 Divide between 4 serving plates and scatter over the Parmesan shavings and pared lemon zest. Serve with salad leaves, if you like.

creamy mushrooms on toasted brioche

Serves 6

Preparation 10 minutes Cooking 6–7 minutes

50g/2oz butter

500g/1lb 2oz mushrooms, such as button, shiitake, oyster and chestnut, sliced if large

1 garlic clove, crushed

6 slices of brioche

142ml/5 fl oz carton of soured cream

1 tbsp chopped fresh dill, plus dill sprigs to garnish

1 Preheat the grill. Heat the butter in a large wok or frying pan and stir-fry the mushrooms and garlic over a fairly high heat for 4–5 minutes until soft, then season.

2 Meanwhile, toast the brioche on both sides; transfer to serving plates.

3 Stir the soured cream and chopped dill into the mushrooms and cook for 2 minutes more until bubbling.

4 Serve at once, spooned over the toasted brioche, garnished with a dill sprig.

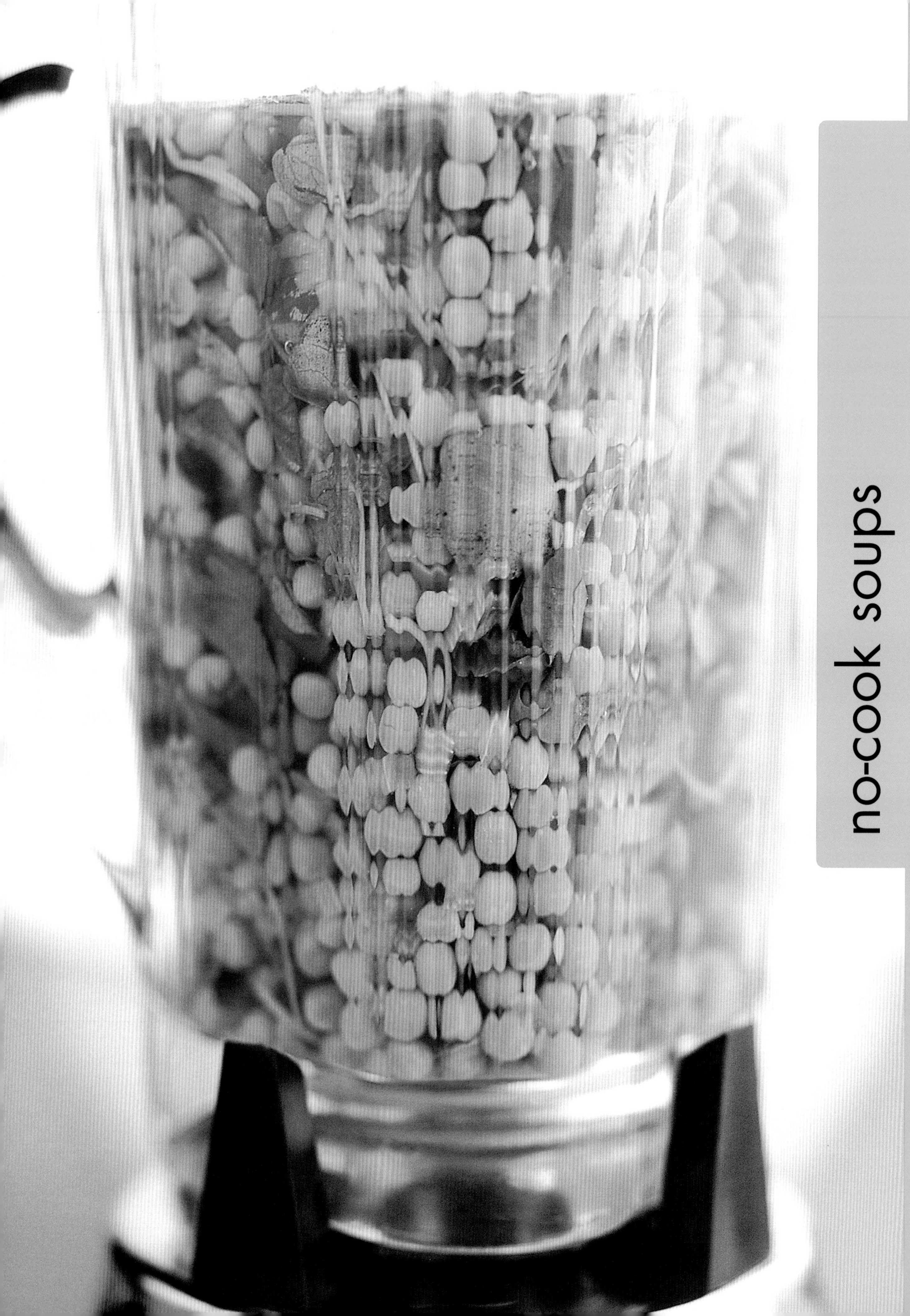

no-cook soups

All you need is a **blender** or **food processor** and some good **flavoursome ripe veg** and you can make yourself a range of interesting, tasty and nutritious **cold soups in minutes** without even going near the stove, except perhaps to warm it up if you fancy serving it hot.

Ingredients to use: tomatoes are the best candidates, as are a whole variety of tender green leaves, like lettuce, baby spinach, sorrel and watercress. Just **flavour** with a few complementary herbs, give **piquancy** with some chopped onion or spring onions, adjust the **texture** with water (or ice cubes to speed the chilling process) or stock, thick or thin cream or crème fraîche, tomato passata or even puréed tinned cooked beans, and **garnish** with snipped herbs, ready-made croutons or tortilla chips.

Secrets of success: it is important not to over-process the ingredients or you lose a lot of their character and end up with a 'juice' rather than a soup.

Pea and Watercress Soup really couldn't be easier, using 350g/12oz fresh or thawed frozen peas and 85g/3oz watercress, thicker stems removed, processed together with 3 chopped spring onions (white and green parts). Dilute to a soupy consistency with good-quality stock and season to taste. Serve the soup cold or warm it through. If you have the time, cut some pancetta into strips and fry these until golden and crisp, for garnish; alternatively, you can sprinkle the soup with some ready-made bacon bits or packet croutons. Try adding a dash of Worcestershire sauce or some mint leaves if the flavour needs a lift.

Experiment for yourself: try processing some cooked beetroot with sour cream and horseradish for an instant borsch; avocado and tomato with coriander and lime juice for your own **'guacamole soup'**, fresh soft lettuce leaves with some chunks of firm cucumber and sour cream, perhaps with a little mint, or a few bunches of your favourite summer herbs, such as chervil, basil, wild rocket and parsley with cream and a good chicken stock for the most refreshing of taste treats. **Avoid carrots**, though, as their fibrousness comes through if they are not cooked first.

Tomato Salsa Soup is gloriously simple, consisting of about 650g/1½lb tomatoes and 1 small red onion, roughly chopped, pulsed with a good handful of fresh coriander leaves, then mixed with a large carton of tomato passata and a large can of cannellini beans, rinsed and drained. You could turn this into a **Tortilla Soup**, which is more like a 'Bloody Mary' soup, spiked with Tabasco sauce, lime juice and ground cumin, thickened with crumbled taco shells and served with more taco shells and ready-made guacamole dip as a dressing. Instead of being stirred in, sour cream is mixed with chopped coriander and swirled through the soup just before serving.

lettuce soup

Serves 6–8

Preparation 10 minutes Cooking 25 minutes

Use a soft-leafed English lettuce, such as Butterhead, for the best colour. Lighter-coloured lettuces, like Iceberg, give a paler soup.

25g/1oz butter
1 onion, chopped
2 medium potatoes, peeled
  and chopped
1 garlic clove
450ml/¾ pint vegetable stock
2 fresh home-grown lettuces,
  finely shredded
225ml/8fl oz milk
salt and pepper
a little freshly grated nutmeg
double cream and chives, to serve

1 Melt the butter in a large casserole with a lid, then stir in the onion, potato and garlic. Add the stock, season and simmer for 20 minutes, covered, until the potato is tender.

2 Add the lettuce and cook, covered, for 3–4 minutes, until the stock returns to the boil and the lettuces are semi-wilted. Be careful not to overcook, or the green freshness will be lost.

3 Liquidize in a food processor or blender, then return to the pan with the milk. Season, add a pinch of nutmeg and serve with some cream floated on top and scattered with snipped chives and a few whole chive stalks.

curried sweet potato soup

Preparation 15 minutes Cooking about 25 minutes

Make a double quantity of this soup and put half in the freezer for another day – it makes a really useful standby supper and can be frozen for up to 3 months. Use orange-fleshed sweet potatoes if you can to give the soup a wonderful colour.

1 tbsp vegetable oil
1 onion, chopped
2 garlic cloves, crushed
2 tbsp curry paste
2 large sweet potatoes, roughly chopped
1 large courgette, chopped
4 tomatoes, chopped
1 litre/1¾ pints vegetable stock
1 large banana, chopped
2 small naan breads, to serve
fresh coriander leaves, to garnish

1. Heat the oil in a large pan and fry the onion for 2–3 minutes until soft. Add the garlic and fry for 2–3 minutes more. Stir in the curry paste and fry that for 2–3 minutes.
2. Add the sweet potatoes, courgettes and tomatoes, and fry for 2–3 minutes, stirring, to coat in the curried mixture.
3. Pour in the stock and bring to the boil. Cover and leave to simmer for 10 minutes. Add the chopped banana about halfway through. Preheat the grill to high.
4. Remove the soup from the heat and blend with a hand blender until smooth. Season to taste and return to the heat to warm through.
5. Meanwhile, lightly toast the bread, then slice it into 4cm/1½ inch strips. Ladle the soup into serving bowls and arrange the naan strips on top. Garnish with coriander leaves to serve.

spinach soup with crunchy garlic bread

Serves 4–6

Preparation 10 minutes Cooking 20 minutes

1 tbsp olive oil
1 onion, finely chopped
500g/1lb 2oz packet of frozen spinach
600ml/1 pint hot vegetable stock
salt and pepper
½–1 tsp freshly grated nutmeg, plus extra for sprinkling
284ml/10fl oz carton of single cream
4 tbsp crème fraîche, to serve

for the garlic bread
50g/2oz softened butter
1 garlic clove, finely chopped
1 small thin baguette, sliced thinly at an angle

1. First make the garlic bread: preheat the oven to 200°C/400°F/Gas 6. Mix the butter and garlic. Put the bread slices on a baking sheet, spread them with the mixture and bake for 10–15 minutes until golden.
2. Meanwhile, heat the oil in a large pan. Add the onion and cook for 5 minutes until golden brown, then add the spinach and stock. Bring to the boil, reduce the heat and simmer for 5 minutes. Pour into a blender or food processor and whiz until smooth (in batches, if necessary).
3. Return to the pan and season to taste. Stir in the nutmeg and cream and heat gently – don't let it boil or the cream will curdle.
4. Pour into warmed bowls, top with crème fraîche and a sprinkling of nutmeg, and serve with the garlic bread.

courgette, basil and brie soup

Preparation 10 minutes Cooking 40 minutes

25g/1oz butter
250g/9oz onion, finely chopped
200g/7oz potato, peeled and cubed
1 garlic clove, finely chopped
splash of white wine
300ml/½ pint vegetable stock
550g/1¼ lb courgettes, chopped
200ml/7fl oz milk
200g/7oz Brie, plus extra slices
    to garnish (optional)
3 tbsp double cream
15 basil leaves, torn, plus extra
    to garnish
salt and pepper

1 Melt the butter in a heavy-based pan and fry the onion for 2–3 minutes until softened. Add the potato, garlic and wine, and cook for a further 5 minutes.

2 Stir in the stock and courgettes and bring to the boil. Reduce the heat, then cover and simmer gently for 20 minutes or until the potato is cooked.

3 Pour in the milk, add the Brie and heat through gently until melted.

4 Stir in the cream and basil, and warm through without letting it boil.

5 Season and serve with extra slices of Brie on top if you like, and sprinkled with basil.

las vegas gumbo

Serves 4–6

Preparation 15 minutes Cooking 30 minutes

50g/2oz butter
2 slices of smoked bacon, chopped
1 large skinless chicken breast,
    sliced
1 small onion, chopped
½ leek, chopped
1 garlic clove, crushed
½ tsp caraway seeds
¼ tsp cayenne pepper
pinch of saffron threads
1 tbsp brandy
2 tsp plain flour
1 tbsp tomato purée
1.2 litres/2 pints chicken or
    vegetable stock
85g/3oz basmati rice
50g/2oz peeled cooked prawns
2 tsp chopped parsley
4 tbsp double cream
½ tsp pepper
crème fraîche, to serve
4–6 cooked prawns in their shells,
    to garnish (optional)

1 Melt the butter in a large pan and add the bacon, chicken, onion, leek, garlic, caraway seeds and cayenne. Fry, stirring, for 8–10 minutes until golden.

2 Add the saffron and brandy, then stir in the flour and tomato purée. Cook gently for 5 minutes. Stir in the stock slowly and bring to the boil. Add the rice, then reduce the heat and simmer gently for 15 minutes, or until the rice is cooked.

3 Remove from the heat and stir in the prawns, parsley and cream. Season with the pepper. Serve with a dollop of crème fraîche, a cooked prawn if you like and an additional sprinkling of pepper.

black bean broth with soba noodles

Preparation 10 minutes Cooking 10 minutes

The nutty flavour of Japanese soba noodles makes them perfect in this vividly flavoured broth, with sharp leafy greens, plus zippy chilli and ginger to revitalize your senses. Oriental noodles and black bean sauce are now widely available from better health-food shops and supermarket chains.

250g/9oz soba noodles

400g/14oz spring greens or green cabbage, finely shredded

3 tbsp vegetable oil

bunch of spring onions, cut into 2cm/¾inch lengths

2 garlic cloves, sliced

¼ tsp dried chilli flakes

3cm/1¼inch piece of fresh root ginger, grated

2 tsp soy sauce

160g/5½oz black bean sauce

600ml/1 pint vegetable stock

100g/4oz cashew nuts, lightly toasted

sesame seeds, to garnish

① Cook the noodles in plenty of boiling water for about 5 minutes until just tender. Add the shredded spring greens or cabbage. Cook for a further 30 seconds, then drain and set aside to keep warm.

② Heat the oil in a medium-sized pan. Add the spring onions and cook gently for 2 minutes. Add the garlic, chilli flakes, ginger, soy sauce, black bean sauce and stock. Bring to the boil, reduce the heat and simmer gently for 3 minutes. Stir in the cashew nuts.

③ Spoon the noodles and spring greens or cabbage into deep bowls. Ladle over the black bean mixture and serve garnished with sesame seeds.

tofu miso soup

Serves 4–6

Preparation 10 minutes Cooking 5 minutes

This is perfect for a light lunch as well as a starter. Use a coarse tofu, as its texture is softer and works best in dishes that are heated gently. Also, the open texture absorbs the other flavours straight away. Tofu and miso paste are now widely available from better health-food shops and supermarket chains.

1.5 litres /2¾ pints vegetable stock

75g/2¾oz somen noodles (thin wheat noodles), or any egg-style noodle

2 leeks, chopped

140g/5oz Chinese or sprouting broccoli, roughly chopped

3 tbsp dark miso paste

5cm/2 inch piece of fresh root ginger, shredded

200g/7oz coarse tofu, cut into cubes

6 tbsp chopped fresh coriander

4 spring onions, sliced

1 tbsp dark soy sauce, to serve

① Bring the stock to the boil in a large pan. Reduce the heat, add the noodles, leeks and broccoli, and simmer for 1 minute.

② Mix the miso to a smooth thin paste with 6 tablespoons of the simmering stock and stir back into the pan. Add the ginger, stir and simmer for a further 3 minutes.

③ Divide the tofu between 4–6 large soup bowls and top each with half the coriander and half the spring onions. Ladle the noodle and vegetable broth over the tofu. Scatter over the remainder of the coriander and spring onions and add a splash of soy sauce to serve.

2

With the emphasis on freshness and easy eating as well as speed, here are some fast but filling ideas with lots of eye and palate appeal – from elegant and intriguing salads to fun-to-eat wraps, Italian chicken-breast 'burgers', quick risotto and a round-up of some more unusual and exciting 'things on toast'.

lightning light meals and brunches

marinated peppers and chillies in oil

Preparation 10 minutes Cooking 10 minutes

Remember that these need to stand for at least 2 days. Keep the jars in a cool dark place, for adding to all sorts of starters, salads, pasta and rice dishes. Stored this way, the contents of the jars keep for 2–3 weeks (the oil will solidify in the fridge). Any leftover oil transforms salad dressings.

6 peppers, preferably mixed
   red, orange and yellow
2 large dried red chillies
2 fresh bay leaves
about 500ml/18fl oz extra-virgin
   olive oil

1 Preheat the grill to high. Quarter the peppers, deseed them and lay them, skin-side up, in the grill pan. Grill for 5–10 minutes, until the skin begins to blister and blacken.

2 Seal the peppers in a plastic food bag. Leave until cool enough to handle, then peel off the skins (this steaming makes the skins come away more easily).

3 Pierce the chillies here and there with a sharp knife and tear the bay leaves slightly to release a little of their oils. Put the chillies and bay leaves in a bowl with the peppers. Pour in olive oil to cover and leave until cold.

4 Tightly pack the peppers, chillies and bay leaves into sterilized dry jars to the neck, then top up with the oil you poured over, adding more if necessary so the peppers are well covered. Secure with the lid, and leave for at least 2 days before use.

marinated peppers with prosciutto and pine nuts

Preparation 10 minutes

Using the marinated peppers above, you can make an instant no-cook Italian-style starter or salad. If you haven't had the time to make the marinated peppers, simply prepare one red, one yellow and one orange pepper following the recipe above up to the end of step 2. Then continue as below, using extra-virgin olive oil for the dressing.

12 pieces of marinated pepper,
   cut into strips, plus 3 tbsp of
   the marinade oil (see above)
1 tbsp fresh lemon juice or 2 tbsp
   balsamic vinegar
12 slices of prosciutto
50g/2oz pine nuts, toasted
1 packet of fresh rocket leaves

1 Mix together the marinade oil and the lemon juice or vinegar and toss with the pepper strips.

2 Arrange the prosciutto slices on plates and scatter over the pepper strips. Sprinkle with the pine nuts and top with a handful of rocket.

mediterranean rice salad

This salad makes an excellent light supper for 4 people, or serve it as an accompaniment to grilled chicken or lamb for 6 people.

2 good-quality vegetable stock cubes
200g/8oz long-grain rice
300g/10oz (about 3) courgettes
1 garlic clove, finely chopped
4 tbsp olive oil
finely grated zest and juice of 1 lemon
½ red onion, thinly sliced
4 tomatoes, cut into wedges
100g/4oz pitted black olives
small handful of fresh mint,
   roughly chopped
salt and pepper
100g/4oz feta
warm pitta bread, to serve

❶ Add the stock cubes to 850ml/1½ pints of boiling water in a large pan and stir until the cubes have dissolved. Tip in the rice, stir well and cook for 10–12 minutes, until the rice is just tender. Drain.

❷ While the rice is cooking, thinly slice the courgettes and put in a serving bowl with the chopped garlic, olive oil, grated lemon zest and juice, the red onion, tomatoes, black olives and mint. Season with salt and pepper and stir everything together thoroughly.

❸ Mix the rice into the vegetables in the bowl. Crumble over the feta and serve warm or cold with warm pitta bread.

prêt's tuna mayo pasta salad

This is one of the most popular lunches at the sandwich chain Prêt à Manger – its 80 stores nationwide make it fresh daily.

250g/9oz fusilli pasta
1 small red onion
1 red pepper
1 green pepper
20 pitted black olives
1 tbsp capers
½ cucumber, sliced
6 generous tbsp mayonnaise
3 tbsp fresh lemon juice
200g/7oz can of tuna, drained
    and flaked

1 Cook the pasta in a pan of boiling salted water according to the packet instructions until just *al dente*; drain, cool under cold running water and drain well again.

2 While the pasta is cooking and cooling, slice the onion thinly and deseed and slice the peppers.

3 Put the drained pasta in a serving bowl and toss with the onion, peppers, black olives, capers and cucumber. (You can make this up to this point a day ahead.)

4 Mix together the mayonnaise and lemon juice, then gently mix into the pasta salad with the tuna.

broad bean, feta and radicchio salad

Packed with punchy flavours, this is a colourful salad that's quick and easy to prepare and, when served with crusty garlic bread, makes a satisfying main course. If you find the broad beans bitter, try pinching off the skin once they are blanched and cooled – it's well worth the effort.

300g/10oz frozen broad beans
salt and pepper
250g/9oz dried casareccia pasta
    (rolled pasta quills), or any
    short pasta
3 tbsp olive oil
2 garlic cloves, crushed
2 tbsp fresh thyme, chopped
200g/7oz semi-dried tomatoes,
    drained if in oil
200g/7oz ready-to-eat dried
    apricots, sliced
1 tbsp red wine vinegar
½ large head of radicchio, leaves
    separated and roughly torn
140g/5oz feta cheese, cubed
50g/2oz pine nuts, toasted

1 Cook the beans in a large pan of lightly salted boiling water for 2 minutes. Remove with a slotted spoon and set aside. Bring the water back to the boil, add the pasta and cook according to the packet instructions until just *al dente*. Drain, refresh in cold water and set aside.

2 While the beans and pasta are cooking, place the broad beans in a large pan with olive oil, garlic and thyme and heat through gently for 10 minutes. Remove from the heat, add the semi-dried tomatoes and apricots and stir in the vinegar. Season well and add the radicchio.

3 Toss the bean mixture and pasta together and season. Divide between 4 plates and scatter over the feta and nuts.

olive pesto pasta

Preparation 10 minutes Cooking 10–12 minutes

350g/12oz pappardelle or tagliatelle
salt and pepper
350g/12oz can of pitted black olives
1 small garlic clove
small bunch of flat-leaf parsley
50g/2oz blanched almonds
3 tbsp olive oil, plus more for
  drizzling
warm focaccia bread, to serve

1 Add the pasta to a large pan of boiling salted water, then return to the boil and cook for 10–12 minutes, until just *al dente*.

2 While the pasta is cooking, drain the olives and put in a food processor with the garlic, parsley and almonds. Whiz until fine, but still with a bit of texture. Stir in the oil.

3 Drain the pasta, reserving 3 tablespoons of the water, and return the pasta to the pan. Stir in the olive mixture and reserved water. Season and drizzle with olive oil.

4 Serve with warm focaccia.

roasted asparagus and tomato thai salad

Give your taste buds a lift with this unusual salad that combines all the wonderful textures and flavours of roasted vegetables with a zingy, Thai-style noodle salad.

400g/14oz asparagus, cut into
   3cm/1½ inch lengths
500g/1lb 2oz cherry tomatoes
250g/9oz shiitake mushrooms,
   thickly sliced
5cm/2 inch piece of fresh root
   ginger, finely chopped
4 Kaffir lime leaves, shredded
4 tbsp groundnut oil
250g/9oz medium egg noodles
bunch of fresh basil, separated
   into leaves

for the dressing
5cm/2 inch piece of lemon grass,
   tough outer leaves discarded
   and finely shredded
1 garlic clove, chopped
3 tbsp groundnut oil
1 tbsp rice vinegar
1 tsp light muscovado sugar
3 tbsp light soy sauce
1 tbsp chilli sauce
3 tbsp chopped fresh coriander
salt and pepper

① Preheat the oven to 230°C/450°F/Gas 8. Place the vegetables in a large roasting tin. Add the ginger and Kaffir leaves, drizzle over the oil, season and stir well. Roast for 20 minutes until tender.

② Meanwhile, cook the noodles according to the packet instructions until just tender. Drain and refresh in cold water.

③ Prepare the dressing: pound the lemon grass and garlic to a paste using a pestle and mortar and spoon into a large bowl. Whisk in the oil and the remaining dressing ingredients.

④ Add the cold, drained noodles and the basil leaves to the dressing, and toss well. Divide between 4 large serving bowls and top with the roasted vegetables and any roasting juices.

skewered lamb with naan bread

Preparation 10 minutes Cooking about 30 minutes

4 neck fillets of lamb, about
    500g/1lb 2oz in total
200g/7oz carton of low-fat
    natural yoghurt
2 tbsp curry paste or powder
1 tbsp sunflower oil
¼ cucumber, peeled and coarsely
    grated
1 garlic clove, crushed
salt and pepper

to serve
shredded Cos lettuce
red onion rings
warmed naan breads

❶ If you are going to barbecue the lamb skewers, get the barbecue going well ahead and soak 8 wooden skewers in cold water for 15 minutes to stop them burning (this is not necessary if you are cooking under the grill, but do preheat the grill).
❷ In a shallow dish, mix half the yoghurt with the curry paste or powder, then turn the lamb fillets in the yoghurt paste to coat them all over. Thread 2 wooden skewers lengthwise through each lamb fillet.
❸ Heat the oil in a pan, add the lamb and cook under a medium-to-high heat for 5 minutes to brown them, turning occasionally. Then lower the heat, cover with a sheet of foil and cook for a further 20–25 minutes, turning occasionally, until tender. Or lay the skewers on the barbecue and cook for 25–30 minutes, turning occasionally.
❹ In a serving bowl, mix the remaining yoghurt with the cucumber and garlic, and season with salt and pepper.
❺ Arrange beds of shredded lettuce and onion rings on each of 4 plates, arrange a lamb skewer on each and pour over the cooking juices. Serve with the warm bread and the yoghurt sauce.

italian burgers

Preparation 10 minutes Cooking about 10 minutes

1 small red onion
small bowlful of iced water
4 chicken breast fillets
salt and pepper
1 tbsp sunflower oil
2 tomatoes
1 ciabatta loaf
1 tbsp pesto, plus more for serving
4 tbsp mayonnaise, plus more for
    serving
shredded Iceberg lettuce

❶ Slice the onion and soak in the iced water. Place the chicken breasts between layers of plastic film and beat with a rolling pin (to make them cook quicker); sprinkle with salt and pepper.
❷ Heat the sunflower oil in a non-stick pan and cook the chicken for 3–4 minutes on each side, until golden.
❸ Meanwhile, slice the tomatoes and cut the ciabatta loaf into 4, then split each piece. Mix the pesto with the mayonnaise and spread a little on 4 ciabatta bottom halves.
❹ To serve: top each of these with shredded lettuce, tomato and a chicken piece. Spoon over more pesto, mayonnaise and the drained onion; top with the other piece of ciabatta.

tuna, bean and sweetcorn salad

Serves 2

185g/6½oz can of tuna chunks,
  drained
165g/5½oz can of sweetcorn with
  peppers, drained
½ red onion, finely chopped
200g/7oz can of red kidney beans,
  drained
salt and pepper
2 handfuls of mixed salad leaves
1 tbsp olive oil
2 tsp lemon juice
pinch of mild chilli powder
toasted crusty bread, to serve

1. In a large bowl, mix the tuna lightly with the sweetcorn, onion and kidney beans. Season well.
2. Divide the salad leaves between 2 plates, season lightly, then pile the tuna salad on top.
3. Drizzle over the olive oil and lemon juice, and sprinkle with the chilli.
4. Serve with toasted crusty bread.

chicken liver, bacon and mushroom toasts

Serves 2

For tender chicken livers it is best to get the pan to a high heat, add the livers in a single layer, leave them for a couple of minutes to brown, then flip them over and cook for another minute. They should be brown on the outside, pink in the middle.

2 slices of smoked streaky bacon,
  rind removed
2 large flat field mushrooms
200g/7oz fresh chicken livers
2 spring onions
25g/1oz butter
2 thick slices of bread
1 tbsp Dijon mustard
3 tbsp crème fraîche
salt and pepper

1. Snip the bacon into short strips and chop the mushrooms into large chunks. Trim any stringy bits from the chicken livers and cut the livers into bite-sized pieces. Slice the spring onions.
2. Melt the butter in a frying pan. Add the bacon strips and cook, stirring, for 5 minutes until they begin to brown. Stir in the chopped mushrooms and continue to cook over a high heat for a further 3 minutes until the mushrooms soften and start to brown. Push the mushrooms and bacon to one side in the pan.
3. Add the chicken livers to the frying pan and cook for 2–3 minutes, stirring, until just cooked (see above). Meanwhile toast the bread.
4. Remove the pan from the heat, stir in the mustard and crème fraîche, and mix well. Season to taste.
5. Spoon the creamy chicken livers, bacon and mushrooms over the hot toast and serve.

chicory, bean and chilli crostini

This is a modern version of beans on toast. Try it topped with stir-fried garlicky greens or cavolo nero (black cabbage) for a change.

2 tbsp olive oil

1 red onion, halved and thinly sliced

2 garlic cloves, thinly sliced

1 red chilli, halved lengthwise, deseeded and thinly sliced

2 tbsp balsamic vinegar

420g/15oz can of cannellini beans, drained and rinsed

2 tbsp dry white wine

15g/½oz fresh flat-leaf parsley, roughly torn

salt and pepper

4 thick slices of crusty Italian bread

2 heads of red chicory, halved lengthwise

1 Heat 1 tablespoon of the olive oil in a large frying pan and fry the onion, garlic and chilli for 5 minutes, until the onion has softened.

2 Stir in the balsamic vinegar, cannellini beans and wine, then cook for a further 3–4 minutes, until all the liquid has evaporated. Stir in the parsley and season to taste.

3 While this is cooking, brush the remaining olive oil over a griddle and heat until it starts to smoke. Add the slices of bread and the chicory, both cut-side down, and cook for 1 minute. Remove the chicory from the griddle. Leave the bread, turn over and cook for a further minute.

4 Place a slice of bread on each of 4 individual serving plates and spoon over the hot bean mixture. Arrange the chicory on top and season with freshly ground black pepper.

croque-monsieur

Serves 1 (easily multiplied)

butter, for spreading

2 thick slices of crusty bread

2–3 slices of wafer-thin ham

25g/1oz Gruyère or Cheddar cheese, grated

4 tsp freshly grated Parmesan

for the lamb's lettuce and sesame salad

handful of lamb's lettuce leaves

2 tsp olive oil

1 tsp lemon juice

salt and pepper

a few toasted sesame seeds

1 Preheat a moderate grill. Butter the bread and make a sandwich with the ham and Gruyère or Cheddar. Press down firmly.

2 Spread more butter over the top of the sandwich and sprinkle with half the Parmesan, then toast under the grill until the bread is crisp and the cheese browned. Repeat on the other side.

3 While it grills, make the salad: put the lamb's lettuce leaves in a bowl. Drizzle over the olive oil and lemon juice. Sprinkle with salt and pepper and toss the leaves thoroughly in the dressing. Sprinkle over the toasted sesame seeds.

4 Serve the croque-monsieur hot, with the lamb's lettuce and sesame salad.

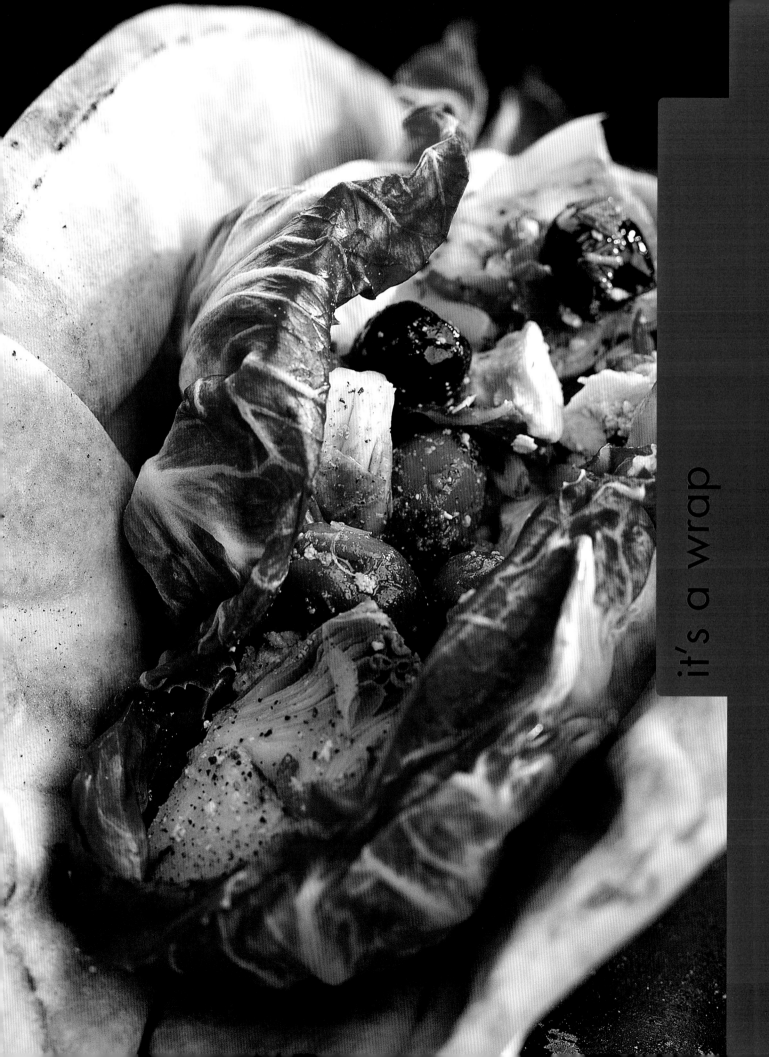

it's a wrap

Wraps are today's healthier and more flexible version of the pasty – ways of making a wide selection of food portable. As well as being **great picnic or lunch-box food**, they can also be made into **starters or light meals** in their own right. If you're serving wraps at the table, they can be made even quicker, easier and lots more fun by setting out the ingredients in separate bowls and then letting people 'roll their own'. Any number of combinations of ingredients can be wrapped in **pitta bread**, **tortillas** or **rice papers**, taking your inspiration from around the world.

Chicken Tortilla Pouches, for instance, contain a filling of sautéed red and yellow peppers and onions with seared chicken breast strips, shredded Little Gem lettuce and soured cream or Greek yoghurt. **Chilli Bean Tortillas** (not illustrated), on the other hand, feature minced beef or lamb flavoured with onion, cumin and chilli powder, browned and cooked with a can each of chopped tomatoes and red kidney beans until tender (about 30 minutes). Each warmed tortilla is topped with some shredded Iceberg lettuce, some chilli mince spooned over that, some grated Cheddar cheese sprinkled on top and the whole thing finished with a little soured cream and a squeeze of lemon juice. You could try other fillings, like a guacamole and tomato salsa, or even plain old baked beans and mayonnaise.

Lemon, Artichoke and Feta Khobez (opposite) use the Moroccan version of pitta bread, while the filling consists of a mix of chopped radicchio, crumbled feta cheese, marinated pitted olives, finely grated preserved lemon, bottled marinated grilled artichokes or antipasti in olive oil, drained, and lots of chopped fresh mint. The whole thing is seasoned with some chopped chilli, garlic and fennel seeds that have been sautéed for a minute or two in lemon oil. Khobez, preserved lemons and lemon oil are available from some large supermarkets and better delis, but you can use ordinary large pitta breads, lemon zest and a fruity olive oil for a very good alternative.

Haloumi and Tomato Wraps need you to grill some thick slices of haloumi cheese until just golden. While they are grilling, toss some shredded Cos lettuce, plum tomato slices, thinly sliced sweet onion rings and chopped fresh mint with a little olive oil and some seasoning. Tuck the cheese and salad inside the warmed pitta pockets and eat immediately.

scrambled smokies

Preparation 10 minutes Cooking about 5 minutes

These are ideal for a lazy weekend brunch. If you haven't got a microwave cooker, you can simply poach the fish in a little milk.

175g/6oz smoked haddock fillet
knob of butter
5 eggs
splash of milk
handful of watercress sprigs,
   larger stalks removed
salt and pepper
2 English muffins, split

1 Put the smoked haddock on a plate, top with half the butter, loosely cover with microwave-proof film then cook in the microwave for 2 minutes on High, until the haddock is cooked. Set aside to cool slightly. Preheat the grill.
2 Crack the eggs into a microwave-proof bowl and whisk with a fork. Stir in the remaining butter and the milk. Cook in the microwave for 2½ minutes, stirring 3 or 4 times during cooking time, using a fork to break up the egg. Alternatively, put in a pan and cook stirring, until the eggs are scrambled.
3 Toast the muffins on both sides until golden. Meanwhile, flake the fish, discarding the skin.
4 When the eggs are cooked, stir in the watercress and flaked fish – the heat from the egg will make the watercress wilt slightly.
5 Spoon some egg mixture on top of each muffin and serve immediately.

quick microwave fish risotto

Preparation 10 minutes Cooking 17 minutes

1 onion
1 garlic clove
1 good-quality vegetable or fish
   stock cube
850ml/1½ pints boiling water
250g/9oz risotto rice, such as
   Arborio, Carnaroli or Vialone Nano
250g/9oz smoked cod or haddock,
   skinned and cut into chunks
large cupful of frozen peas
large knob of butter
1 lemon, cut into 8 wedges
salt and pepper

1 Finely chop the onion and garlic and put them in a large bowl with the stock cube and 300ml/½ pint of the boiling water. Stir well, then cover and microwave on High for 3 minutes.
2 Stir in the rice with another 300ml/½ pint of boiling water, cover and microwave on High for 10 minutes, stirring after 5 minutes.
3 Stir the fish into the rice together with the frozen peas and remaining boiling water. Cover and microwave on High for 4 minutes. Check the rice is cooked – if not, microwave for another minute.
4 Leave to stand for 1–2 minutes, to allow the liquid to be absorbed, then stir in the butter, a little salt if necessary (there is probably enough from the stock and fish) and lots of freshly ground black pepper.
5 Serve hot, with lemon wedges.

minted pea omelette

Serves 2

Preparation 10 minutes Cooking about 10 minutes

5 eggs
1 tbsp chopped fresh mint
85g/3oz frozen peas
salt and pepper
knob of butter
50g/2oz grated Cheddar cheese
crusty white bread and a green
   salad, to serve

① Preheat the grill. In a bowl, lightly beat the eggs with a fork until just frothy. Stir in the mint and the peas, and season with salt and pepper.

② Heat the butter in a frying pan, swirling it round so it coats the base and sides. When it starts to froth, pour in the egg mixture, swirling the pan to spread it evenly. Cook over a moderate heat for 3–4 minutes, until almost set but the surface is still a bit liquid.

③ Sprinkle over the cheese, then grill for 2–3 minutes, until the cheese has melted.

④ Tilt the pan on to the edge of the plate, then, with a fork, fold the omelette in half and slide on to the plate. Cut in half and serve with crusty white bread and a green salad.

souffléed olive and avocado omelette

Serves 1

Preparation 5 minutes Cooking 5 minutes

This is perfect when you feel like something a little indulgent during a quiet night in. Serve it with a simple tomato salad.

3 medium eggs, separated
1 tbsp milk
2 tbsp chopped fresh flat-leaf
   parsley
2 tsp olive oil
2 tbsp black olive tapenade
1 small avocado, halved, stoned
   and sliced
juice of ½ lemon
salt and pepper

① Preheat the grill to high. Place the egg whites in a large bowl and whisk to soft peaks. Place the egg yolks in a separate bowl with the milk and parsley. Season and beat together. Add a quarter of the whites to the yolks and gently stir. Gently fold in the remaining egg whites.

② Heat the oil in a 20cm/8 inch non-stick frying pan. Add the egg mixture and cook for 2–3 minutes until lightly set.

③ Place under the grill for 1–2 minutes to cook the top.

④ Spoon the olive tapenade over one half of the omelette. Top with the avocado and squeeze over the lemon juice. Fold over the other half, transfer to a plate and serve with a tomato salad, if you like.

great american brunch

4 tbsp olive oil

700g/1lb 9 oz cooked waxy potatoes, chopped into small cubes

1 onion, finely chopped

200g/8oz cooked beetroot, fresh or vacuum-packed (not in vinegar), peeled and cut into small pieces

200g/8oz thickly sliced cooked ham, torn into strips

4 tbsp soured cream

2 tsp horseradish sauce

salt and pepper

4 eggs

1 Heat half the oil in a large pan and fry the potatoes for 3–4 minutes over a high heat until browned; fry the onion for 5 minutes until lightly coloured. Stir in the beetroot and ham. Cook for 5 minutes more, until the ingredients are all piping hot.

2 In a bowl, mix the soured cream and horseradish with salt and pepper to taste.

3 Heat the remaining oil in another pan and fry the eggs how you like them.

4 Divide the ham hash between plates, top with a fried egg and serve with a little horseradish cream.

Variations
You could use cooked turkey or chicken instead of the ham.

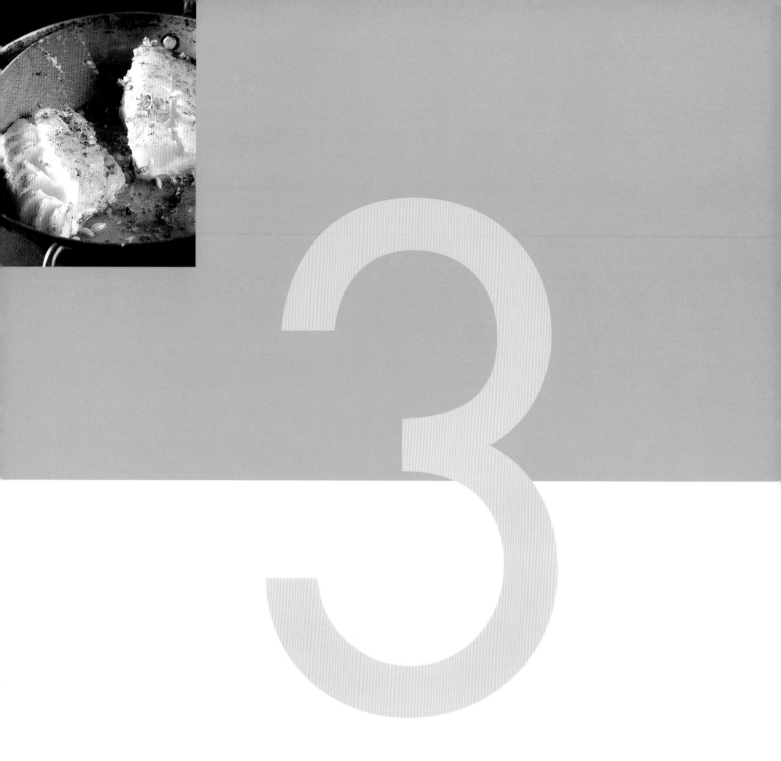

3

Those regular weekly evening meals really seem to eat up the time, so it's all too tempting to fall back on habitual old favourites or expensive convenience food night after night. To help you come up with something new, here are dishes that will please all the family and yet still be ready on time with the minimum of fuss.

fast family fare

cod with lemon and parsley sauce

Serves 2

Preparation 10 minutes Cooking 10 minutes

Fish is perfect for those making meals in a hurry. It cooks quickly, you can get it ready-prepared and it lends itself to many very simple but tasty treatments. White fish fillets are particularly versatile and, of course, frozen they make great stand-bys.

2 cod fillets, each about 175g/6oz

flour, for dusting

salt and pepper

25g/1oz butter

juice of 1 lemon

1 heaped tbsp chopped parsley

1 Coat the cod fillets in the seasoned flour, dusting off any excess.

2 Heat half the butter in a frying pan. When it is bubbling, add the fish fillets and cook them over a fairly high heat until the undersides are nicely browned.

3 Using a fish slice, turn the fillets carefully and brown the other sides. When the fish is just cooked (the flesh will start to flake and become opaque), add the remaining butter to the pan. When it is bubbling, stir in the lemon juice, salt and pepper. Bubble the sauce up until slightly thickened, then stir in the parsley.

4 Serve with new potatoes and French or runner beans.

cheese and mustard crusted cod

Preparation 5 minutes Cooking 20 minutes

salt and pepper

4 pieces of skinned cod fillet, each about 150–175g/5–6oz

175g/6oz mature Cheddar cheese, grated

2 tsp wholegrain mustard

4 tbsp single cream or creamy milk

2 tbsp snipped fresh chives

for the tomato and chive salad

6 tomatoes

2 tbsp snipped fresh chives

1 Preheat the oven to 180°C/350°C/Gas 4. Season the fish and put it in an ovenproof serving dish.

2 Mix the cheese with the mustard, cream and chives, and spread over each cod fillet.

3 Bake for 20 minutes, until the fish is cooked and the top is golden.

4 Make the tomato and chive salad: slice the tomatoes and arrange on 4 plates. Scatter over the chives and season.

5 Serve the fish on the salad, with new potatoes if you like.

crisp mustard cod

Preparation 10 minutes Cooking 8–10 minutes

This topping also works well with salmon fillets.

1 thick slice of white bread
small bunch of parsley
2 tbsp olive oil
finely grated zest of 1 lemon
salt and pepper
4 skinless cod fillets, each about
   100g/4oz
2 rounded tsp mustard, such as
   wholegrain
mayonnaise, to serve

① Preheat the oven to 200°C/400°F/Gas 6. Break up the bread and throw it into a food processor or blender together with the parsley. Whiz to fine crumbs, then drizzle in the oil, add the lemon zest, salt and pepper, and briefly whiz again to mix.

② Put the cod fillets in a shallow ovenproof dish and spread a little mustard over each portion. Press the crumbs on top in an even layer.

③ Bake for 8–10 minutes, until the topping is quite crisp and the cod is cooked through.

④ Serve with a spoonful of mayonnaise, and some steamed new potatoes and broccoli if you like.

crunchy-topped fish pie

Preparation 5 minutes Cooking 45 minutes

Using a ready-made sauce, this great family pie is easy enough for the kids to make.

650g/1½lb skinless cod or haddock
100g/4oz frozen peas
200g/7oz fresh watercress or dill
  and lemon sauce
3 thick slices of bread
25g/1oz butter, melted
85g/3oz mature Cheddar cheese,
  grated

1 Preheat the oven to 190°C/375°F/Gas 5.
2 Cut the fish into chunks and transfer to a pie dish. Sprinkle over the peas, then pour over the sauce and stir lightly.
3 Cut the bread into cubes and toss with the melted butter. Spread over the pie filling and sprinkle with the cheese.
4 Bake for 45 minutes, until the topping is crisp and the fish is tender.

plaice and crispy bacon grill

Preparation 5 minutes Cooking 4–5 minutes

about 30g/1oz butter
4 plaice fillets
salt and pepper
3 slices of smoked back bacon
juice of 1 lemon

1 Preheat the grill. Line a grill pan with a sheet of foil and butter it lightly.
2 Arrange the plaice fillets on the foil in one layer and season with salt and pepper. Cut the bacon into thin strips and scatter over the fish. Top each plaice fillet with a knob of butter and squeeze over some lemon juice.
3 Grill for 4–5 minutes, until the fish is lightly golden and the bacon is crisp.
4 Transfer to serving plates, spoon over the cooking juices and serve with steamed buttered spinach and boiled new potatoes if you like.

Stir-fries really are the way to keep a family well fed in short order. With a good supply of **fresh vegetables** in the fridge and some **oriental noodles** in the storecupboard, you will always have a nutritious and filling meal to hand.

Ingredients to use: the best vegetables for stir-fries include chillies and spring onions for **punch**, red and green peppers, baby sweetcorn, courgettes, broccoli and green beans for **crunch**, and cherry tomatoes and shredded carrots for **colour**. Toss in some chopped herbs, like parsley or coriander, at the end for added **flavour**. Add **protein** by means of prawns, thinly sliced beef, pork, lamb or poultry. Flavourings like ginger, soy sauce and sesame oil (add, sparingly, at the end) give a definite Oriental feel, but Worcestershire sauce, citrus zest and/or juice, as appropriate, can give a different result, as in the prawn dish below.

The secrets of success: good stir-frying is all in the **preparation**; get everything peeled and chopped and the flavourings to hand before you start cooking, and arrange bowlfuls of ingredients that will take roughly the same time to cook so they can be tipped in together.

Chicken and Broccoli Noodles incorporates the noodles for a substantial one-pot meal. Cook 250g/9oz egg noodles in a pan of boiling salted water for 5 minutes, adding 350g/12oz broccoli florets for the last 2 minutes. Drain and rinse well under cold running water until cool.

Meanwhile, heat a wok or frying pan until very hot. Add 2 tablespoons groundnut oil, then stir in 2.5cm/1inch piece of fresh root ginger, grated, and 4 garlic cloves, thinly sliced. Stir-fry for 30 seconds, then add 2 skinless chicken breast fillets cut into thin strips and cook for 5 minutes, stirring often, until the chicken is tinged with brown. Add a bunch of spring onions cut in half horizontally and stir briefly to wilt slightly.

Mix 3 tablespoons soy sauce and 200ml/7fl oz chicken or vegetable stock and stir into the pan. Tip the drained noodles and broccoli into the pan, season with pepper and toss everything together to heat through.

Lemon Prawn Pan-fry stir-fries a deseeded and sliced red pepper with 2 large courgettes, halved lengthwise and sliced, in about 2 tablespoons olive oil for about 3 minutes. Then add 200g/7oz peeled cooked prawns, 1 chopped garlic clove and 100g/4oz frozen peas, and stir-fry together for about 1 minute more. Finally, dress with the grated zest and juice of 1 lemon and some chopped parsley, and serve with rice or noodles.

barbecued coriander chicken with guacamole salsa

Preparation 15 minutes Cooking about 20 minutes

4 skinless chicken breast fillets,
  each about 140g/5oz
2 tbsp olive oil
2 tbsp finely chopped fresh coriander
1 tbsp fresh lemon juice
120g/4oz bag of mixed salad leaves
salt and pepper
garlic bread, to serve

for the guacamole salsa
¼ red onion, roughly chopped
1 garlic clove, quartered
½–1 green chilli, deseeded
2 tomatoes, halved and deseeded
1 large or 2 small ripe avocado(s),
  peeled, stoned and roughly
  chopped
good handful of fresh coriander
1 tbsp fresh lemon juice

1 Preheat the grill or barbecue. Brush the chicken with 1 tablespoon of the olive oil. Season well, then grill or barbecue for 20 minutes, turning halfway through. Sprinkle the coriander over the chicken for the last 5 minutes of cooking.

2 While the chicken cooks, make the salsa: put the onion, garlic and chilli in a food processor and pulse for a few seconds at a time to chop finely. Add the tomatoes, avocado, coriander and lemon juice and pulse until the ingredients are combined, but the mixture still has a chunky texture.

3 When ready to serve: put the salad leaves in a bowl, sprinkle over the remaining oil and the lemon juice and season well with salt and pepper. Toss well to mix, then divide the salad between plates and serve with the chicken, guacamole salsa and garlic bread.

chicken tarragon pasta

Serves 3

Preparation 5–10 minutes Cooking 10–12 minutes

250g/9oz pasta, such as tagliatelle
  or pappardelle
salt and pepper
2 tbsp olive oil
2 skinless chicken breast fillets,
  cut into small pieces
2 garlic cloves, chopped
142ml/5fl oz carton of single cream
3 tbsp roughly chopped fresh
  tarragon leaves
100g/4oz spinach leaves, thick
  stems removed
lemon wedges, to serve

1 Cook the pasta in a large pan of boiling salted water for 8–10 minutes, or according to the packet instructions, until just tender.

2 Meanwhile, heat the oil in a large frying pan, add the chicken and fry over a high heat for 4–5 minutes, stirring often, until golden and cooked.

3 Add the garlic, then stir in the cream, tarragon and 3 tablespoons of the pasta cooking liquid. Heat through over a low heat.

4 When the pasta is cooked, tip the spinach into the same pan and stir well. (It will wilt immediately in the hot water.) Drain the spinach and pasta mixture well, then toss it into the creamy chicken. Season generously with salt and pepper.

5 Serve with lemon wedges for squeezing over.

lamb chop and spicy chip bake

Preparation 5 minutes Cooking about 40 minutes

3 tbsp olive oil

2 large onions, peeled and sliced

750g/1lb 10½oz bag of frozen, hot
  and spicy potato wedges

8 small lamb chops

1 tsp dried thyme

150ml/¼ pint lamb or chicken stock

1 tbsp tomato purée

salt and pepper

1 Preheat the oven to 230°C/450°F/ Gas 8. Heat a large roasting tin on the hob, then add 2 tablespoons of the olive oil.

2 Put the onions in the tin and fry for about 5 minutes, stirring often, until golden. Remove from the heat and scatter over the potato wedges. Put the chops on top, sprinkle over the thyme and drizzle over the remaining oil.

3 Bake for 20 minutes.

4 Mix the stock with the tomato purée and pour around the chops in the tin. Bake for 10 minutes more until everything is brown and crisp.

5 Season and serve.

teriyaki chicken and vegetable bake

Preparation 5–10 minutes Cooking 40–45 minutes

Although you have to attend to this dish in the oven a couple of times during the cooking, using a ready-made teriyaki marinade makes it so easy to prepare that it still keeps within our limit of time needed in the kitchen and gives a wonderfully deep and full-flavoured result.

8 chicken thighs, skin on

125ml/4fl oz ready-made teriyaki
  marinade

2 tsp grated fresh root ginger

1 tbsp clear honey

5 spring onions, finely chopped

2 red peppers, quartered and
  deseeded

3 courgettes, each cut into
  4 lengthwise

boiled or steamed rice, to serve

1 Preheat the oven to 200°C/400°F/Gas 6. Put the chicken thighs in a single layer in a large roasting tin. Mix the teriyaki marinade with the ginger, honey and spring onions, then pour over the chicken, turning the pieces to coat them evenly.

2 Put the chicken in the oven for 25 minutes, turning halfway through.

3 After 25 minutes, add the peppers and courgettes, turning them in the marinade. (Arrange the vegetables around the chicken rather than on top, so the chicken can brown nicely.) Return the roasting tin to the oven for 15–20 minutes until the chicken and vegetables are tender.

4 Serve with the pan juices and rice.

spicy roast chicken

Preparation 10 minutes Cooking 40–45 minutes

4 carrots, about 300g/10oz in total
2 parsnips, about 400g/14oz in total
25g/1oz butter
1 tbsp olive oil
1 tsp ground cumin
1 tsp ground coriander
½ tsp ground turmeric
8 chicken pieces, such as
   drumsticks or thighs
salt and pepper
1 garlic clove, finely chopped
85g/3oz mixed nuts, such as
   almonds, pecans, Brazil nuts,
   hazelnuts and cashews
natural yoghurt and warmed naan
   bread, to serve

❶ Preheat the oven to 200°C/400°F/Gas 6. Cut the carrots and parsnips into evenly-sized sticks.

❷ Heat the butter, oil and spices in a roasting tin on the hob until the butter melts. Season the chicken with salt and pepper and put in the tin. Stir well to coat the chicken. Stir in the garlic and chopped vegetables.

❸ Roast for 40–45 minutes, stirring occasionally, until the chicken and vegetables are browned.

❹ Stir in the nuts for the last 10 minutes of cooking.

❺ Serve with spoonfuls of yoghurt and warmed naan bread.

chinese turkey kebabs with 4-minute noodles

If you're using wooden skewers, soak them in water first for about 30 minutes to prevent them catching fire under the grill.

3 tbsp soy sauce

1 tbsp tomato purée

2 tsp sugar

150ml/¼ pint hot chicken or vegetable stock

450g/1lb turkey breast fillets, cut into strips

250g/9oz packet of medium egg noodles

1 Chinese cabbage, cut into thin strips

100g/4oz sugar snap peas

1. Preheat the grill to high and boil a kettle of water.
2. In a bowl, blend together the soy sauce, tomato purée and sugar, then spoon half into a pan with the stock. Add the turkey to the remaining sauce in the bowl and stir to coat well.
3. Thread the turkey on to 4 skewers (see above) and grill for 6–8 minutes, turning every now and then, until evenly cooked.
4. Meanwhile, break up the noodles and put in a large pan with the cabbage and sugar snap peas. Cover with boiling water, bring to the boil, then simmer for 4 minutes. Bring the tomato sauce and stock mixture to the boil, then simmer gently for a couple of minutes.
5. Drain the noodles and vegetables, then add to the sauce and toss well.
6. Divide between serving plates and place a kebab on top of each.

creamy ham and bean stew

Preparation 10 minutes Cooking about 20 minutes

This is an excellent quick one-pot meal that couldn't be simpler to make.

1 tbsp sunflower oil
1 onion, chopped
3 garlic cloves, crushed
450g/1lb gammon steaks, rind
  removed and diced
1 courgette, sliced
1 red pepper, cored, deseeded
  and chopped
300ml/½ pint hot chicken stock
420g/15oz can of cannellini beans,
  drained
420g/15oz can of butter beans,
  drained
2 tbsp wholegrain mustard
salt and pepper
4 tbsp crème fraîche
2 tbsp chopped fresh parsley
crusty bread and salad, to serve

1 Heat the sunflower oil in a large pan, add the onion and garlic and cook for 3–4 minutes, until the onion has softened.
2 Add the gammon, courgette and red pepper, and fry for 4–5 minutes until the courgette starts to brown.
3 Pour in the chicken stock and bring to the boil. Turn down the heat and simmer for 10 minutes until the ham is cooked through.
4 Stir in the cannellini and butter beans, then the mustard and season with salt and pepper.
5 Remove from the heat and stir in the crème fraîche and parsley.
6 Serve the stew with crusty bread and salad.

creamy spaghetti with bacon and courgette

Preparation 5 minutes Cooking about 10 minutes

1 tbsp olive oil, plus more for serving
6 slices of streaky bacon, rind
  removed and cut into strips
2 courgettes, cut into sticks
500g/1lb 2oz fresh spaghetti
salt and pepper
80g/3oz Boursin or Le Roulé cheese
142ml/5fl oz carton of single cream
freshly grated Parmesan, to serve

1 Heat the olive oil in a wide frying pan, then fry the bacon until crisp. Toss in the courgettes and cook for a few more minutes.
2 Meanwhile, cook the pasta in a large pan of boiling salted water for 3 minutes. Drain.
3 Add the creamy cheese and the cream to the bacon and courgettes, and stir to make a sauce.
4 Toss the sauce with the spaghetti and serve with a drizzle of olive oil, some freshly grated Parmesan and lots of freshly ground black pepper.

Variations
You could replace the courgettes with 175g/6oz sliced mushrooms or a chopped deseeded red pepper.

sausage, bacon and bean bake

Serves 6

Preparation 10 minutes Cooking 25–30 minutes

If you can't get cannellini beans, use haricot, pinto or kidney beans instead.

2 tbsp olive oil
12 quality plump herby sausages
1 large onion, cut into wedges
6 rindless streaky bacon, chopped
4 celery stalks, sliced
2 garlic cloves, crushed
600ml/1 pint hot vegetable or
  chicken stock
3 tbsp tomato purée
400g/14oz can of cannellini beans,
  drained
2 tbsp whole-grain mustard
salt and pepper
garlic bread, to serve

1 Preheat the oven to 200°C/400°F/Gas 6. Heat half the oil in a frying pan, then brown the sausages all over. Transfer to a roasting tin.

2 Add the remaining oil to the frying pan, together with the onion, bacon, celery and garlic, and fry until golden.

3 Add the stock, tomato purée and beans, scraping up any bits from the bottom of the pan. Let the stock bubble up, then add to the tin and bake, uncovered, for 15–20 minutes.

4 Remove from the oven and stir in the mustard, season with salt and pepper, and serve hot with garlic bread.

spicy sausage pasta

Preparation 10 minutes Cooking 15–20 minutes

2 tbsp olive oil
6 good-quality sausages
salt
1 onion, finely chopped
1–2 garlic cloves, finely chopped
400g/14oz can of chopped tomatoes
1 tsp dried oregano
350g/12oz penne or rigatoni pasta
1 tbsp red pesto

1 Heat the oil in a frying pan and cook the sausage over a high heat for a few minutes, until well browned all over. Remove from the pan and cut into 2.5cm/1 inch pieces.

2 Meanwhile, bring a large pan of salted water to the boil and while you are cutting up the sausages, fry the onion and garlic in the frying pan for 5 minutes. Add the tomatoes with their liquid, the sausage pieces and the oregano. Cover, reduce the heat and simmer for 10 minutes.

3 At the same time, put the pasta in the pan of boiling water and cook for 10–12 minutes, until just tender.

4 When the sauce has thickened, stir in the pesto. Drain the pasta and return to the pan. Stir in the sauce and serve.

lamb and spring onion stir-fry

Preparation 10 minutes Cooking 2–3 minutes

3 tbsp soy sauce

3 tbsp sherry

3 tbsp sesame oil

3 tbsp vegetable oil

2 tsp wine vinegar

2 garlic cloves, thinly sliced

450g/1lb lamb fillet, sliced thinly
across the grain

bunch of spring onions, cut at an
angle into 5cm/2 inch lengths

boiled or steamed rice, to serve

1 In a bowl, mix together the soy sauce, sherry, sesame oil, vinegar and 4 tablespoons of water.

2 Heat the vegetable oil in a large frying pan or wok, then add the garlic and stir-fry briefly. Add the lamb and stir-fry for 1–2 minutes until browned.

3 Stir in the soy sauce mixture and bubble briefly. Add the spring onions and cook for a few seconds until they just start to soften.

4 Serve with rice.

Variation
You could use chicken or beef instead of lamb.

lamb and date casserole

Preparation 10 minutes Cooking about 30 minutes

This is a really easy one-pot feast. Some supermarkets sell lamb already diced, which is perfect for this dish - otherwise cut up some fillet or leg steaks.

550g/1¼ lb diced lamb

1 tbsp plain flour

2 tbsp olive oil

2 onions, chopped

3 large carrots, cut into chunks

2 garlic cloves, finely chopped

600ml/1 pint chicken, lamb or
vegetable stock

1 tbsp cranberry sauce

2 tsp tomato purée

12 pitted ready-to-eat dates

3 tbsp chopped fresh parsley

salt and pepper

rice or steamed couscous, to serve

1 Put the lamb and flour in a plastic food bag and shake well. Heat the olive oil in a large pan. Remove the lamb and shake off any excess flour, then add the lamb to the pan with the onion and carrots. Cook over a medium-to-high heat for 8–10 minutes, stirring often, until the lamb and onions are golden.

2 Add the garlic and cook for 1 minute. Add the stock and bring to the boil. Reduce the heat and simmer, covered, for 20 minutes, until thickened slightly.

3 Stir in the cranberry sauce, tomato purée, dates, parsley and salt and pepper to taste. Warm through.

4 Serve with rice or couscous.

BLT burgers

Preparation 10 minutes Cooking about 15 minutes

These are woofed down by kids of all ages, from 8 to 80, and are especially nice in summer when you can cook them on the barbecue.

500g/1lb 2oz minced beef
salt and pepper
2 tbsp Worcestershire sauce
4 slices of smoked streaky bacon
2 large tomatoes, sliced
4 large crisp lettuce leaves
4 burger buns
4 tbsp mayonnaise

1 Preheat the grill to hot (or light the barbecue well ahead). Season the mince well and mix in the Worcestershire sauce. Divide the meat into 4 and shape into thickish burgers.

2 Cook for 7–8 minutes on each side (it's safest to ensure minced meat is cooked right through), but be careful not to overcook or they will become dry.

3 After you turn the burgers, cook the bacon alongside them until crisp, turning once. Drain on kitchen paper.

4 Arrange the tomato slices on the bottom halves of the buns, followed by the lettuce leaves. Put the burgers on top, lay a slice of bacon on each and top with a dollop of mayonnaise. Set the other halves of the buns on top.

Variations
Burgers lend themselves to many variations: use minced lamb, pork or turkey instead of beef; try adding some finely chopped red onion and/or some finely chopped parsley to the minced mixture.

beef sukiyaki

Preparation 10 minutes Cooking 10–15 minutes

Sukiyaki is a traditional Japanese way of preparing meat, cut into thin slices, then seared quickly.

250g/9oz Japanese
  or Thai fragrant rice
115g/4oz sugar snap peas
4 spring onions, sliced
450g/1lb sirloin or topside of beef
1 tsp sunflower oil
1 large red pepper, cored, deseeded
  and thickly sliced

for the sukiyaki sauce
3 tbsp light soy sauce
3 tbsp sake, mirin or dry sherry
1 tbsp light muscovado sugar
1 tbsp clear honey
1 tsp chilli sauce

1 Cook the rice in boiling salted water according to the packet instructions until just tender. Add the sugar snap peas and spring onions 3 minutes before the end of cooking time.

2 Meanwhile, make the sukiyaki sauce: put the soy sauce, sake, mirin or sherry and sugar in a small pan and bring to the boil, stirring. Simmer for 1–2 minutes, still stirring, until the sugar has dissolved. Remove from the heat, stir in the honey and set aside.

3 Holding the knife so the blade is flat, cut thin horizontal slices through the whole length of the beef.

4 Preheat a heavy-based frying pan (it is best to use non-stick as you don't need to use so much oil) and brush with the oil. Cook the pepper slices for 4–5 minutes, turning occasionally, until starting to brown, then remove from the pan and keep warm.

5 Cook the strips of the beef in the same pan for 1–2 minutes on each side, until they also start to brown.

6 Drain the rice and vegetables and spoon on to 4 plates. Top with the peppers and beef. Stir the chilli sauce into the sukiyaki sauce and drizzle over.

new mexican chilli

Preparation 10 minutes Cooking 1¼ hours

1 tsp hot chilli powder or 1½ tbsp mild

1 tsp each ground cumin and paprika

1 tsp dried oregano

450g/1lb lean pork, cut into cubes

3 tbsp groundnut or vegetable oil

1 large onion, finely chopped

1 sweet red pepper, cored, deseeded
  and cut into chunks

2 fat garlic cloves, finely chopped

400g/14oz can of chopped tomatoes

2 tbsp tomato purée

1 tbsp light muscovado sugar

150ml/¼ pint chicken stock

150ml/¼ pint red wine

400g/14oz canned pinto or red kidney
  beans, drained

salt

soured cream, to serve

chopped fresh parsley, to garnish

1 Mix together the spices and herbs and toss with the pork. Heat 2 table-spoons of the oil in a pan, add the meat and fry for 2 minutes, then remove.

2 Add the remaining oil, onion, pepper and garlic and fry for 4–5 minutes until golden.

3 Return the meat to the pan and stir in the tomatoes with their liquid, the tomato purée, sugar, stock and wine. Cover and cook gently for 1 hour, until the meat is tender and the stew has the consistency of a chunky soup.

4 Stir in the beans and simmer for 5 minutes.

5 Season with salt, if necessary, and serve with soured cream and garnished with chopped parsley. Serve with rice or bread.

cauliflower cheese lasagne

Preparation 15 minutes Cooking 50 minutes

Don't be put off by the thought of the usual home-made lasagne, using every pan in the kitchen. For this recipe you don't need to make a sauce – just stir some herbs into crème fraîche, and start layering.

250g/9oz cauliflower florets
250g/9oz broccoli florets
salt and pepper
200g/7oz (12 sheets) dried
  'no-precook' lasagne sheets
  or fresh lasagne
500ml/18fl oz carton of crème fraîche
3 tbsp finely chopped fresh parsley
1 tbsp chopped fresh oregano, or
  1 tsp dried olive oil, for brushing
200g/7oz oak-smoked ham, diced
12 cherry tomatoes, halved
200g/7oz mature double Gloucester
  cheese, grated
leafy salad and crusty bread,
  to serve

1 Preheat the oven to180°C/350°F/Gas 4. Lightly cook the cauliflower and broccoli in a pan of boiling salted water for about 5 minutes until just tender.

2 If you're using dried 'no-precook' lasagne, soak it in hot (not boiling) water for about 10 minutes to soften. If using fresh, just use it as it is.

3 Mix the crème fraîche with 3 tablespoons of water and the herbs. Brush an ovenproof dish large enough to take the lasagne sheets with a little oil, and line with one-third of the pasta sheets, followed by half the cauliflower and broccoli, half the ham, half the tomatoes, one-third of the cheese and one-third of the crème fraîche sauce. Repeat the layers, finishing with a layer of pasta. Pour over the remaining sauce and sprinkle with the remaining grated cheese.

4 Bake in the oven for 40 minutes, then increase the oven setting to 190°C/375°F/Gas 5 and bake for 10 minutes more, until golden and bubbling.

5 Serve hot with a leafy salad and fresh crusty bread.

stuffed marrow

Preparation 5 minutes Cooking 25 minutes

4 tbsp olive oil
1 large onion, chopped
3 garlic cloves, finely chopped
two 400g/14oz cans of chopped
  tomatoes
2 tbsp tomato purée
two 400g/14oz cans of butter
  beans, drained and rinsed
85g/3oz ciabatta bread, broken
  into pieces
handful of fresh parsley
salt and pepper
1 marrow, about 1kg/2¼lb

1 Preheat the oven to 200°C/400°F/Gas 6 and put a large pan of water on to heat to the boil.

2 Heat 1 tablespoon of the oil in a saucepan and add the onion. Cook, stirring, for 5 minutes, until softened. Add 2 of the garlic cloves and cook for a further minute.

3 Tip in the chopped tomatoes and the tomato purée, bring to the boil, cover and cook for 15 minutes, until the sauce has thickened, stirring in the beans for the last 2 minutes of the cooking time.

4 Meanwhile, put the ciabatta into a processor with the remaining garlic, oil, parsley leaves and salt and pepper. Pulse until the mixture turns into rough crumbs. Tip on to a baking sheet and bake for 10 minutes until the crumbs are crispy.

5 Peel the marrow, top and tail, then cut into eight 3cm/1¼inch thick slices. Cut out and discard the seeds (for speed, you can take them out with a 5cm/2 inch biscuit cutter). Cook the marrow slices in the boiling salted water for 4 minutes until tender. Drain well, and then transfer to a serving dish.

6 Pile the tomato mixture into the marrow slices, top with the crumbs and serve.

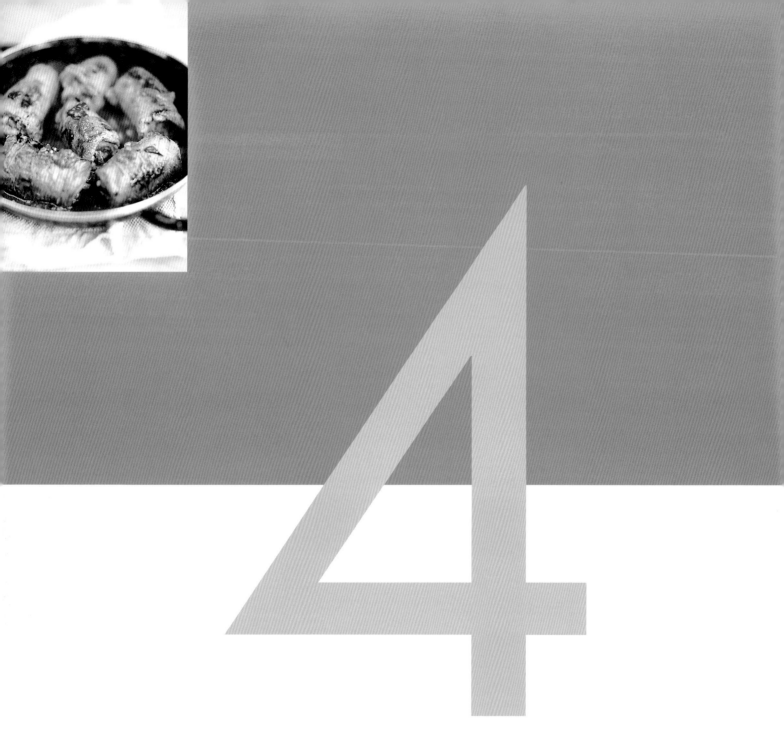

When having people over, it's nice to cook something with a little bit of style. It needn't take much time – perhaps all you need are a few more sophisticated ingredients, like capers, pine nuts or prosciutto, to spark up a basic piece of meat, poultry or fish. The classic trick of adding a splash of wine and some cream always works wonders.

effortless entertaining

lemon and oregano pork

Preparation 5 minutes Cooking 6–8 minutes

If you have the time, you could always make your own breadcrumbs, providing you have some fairly dry bread lying around; grate it or whiz it in the food processor. If some fresh oregano is readily available, this will take this dish up a level to the truly sublime; chop it finely and use just about a heaped tablespoonful.

finely grated zest and juice of
  1 lemon
100g/3½oz ready-made natural-
  coloured breadcrumbs
2 tsp dried oregano
4 pork escalopes
2 tbsp sunflower oil
lemon mayonnaise, to serve

① Mix together the lemon zest, breadcrumbs and oregano on a plate. Pour the lemon juice on to another plate. Dip each pork escalope first into the lemon juice and then into the breadcrumb mixture, until well coated.
② Heat the oil in a large frying pan over a high heat and fry the pork escalopes for 3–4 minutes on each side, until the crumbs are crisp and the pork is cooked through.
③ Serve each escalope with a spoonful of lemon mayonnaise, and some new potatoes and green beans.

rolled pork slices (*braciole di maiale*)

Serves 6

Preparation 10 minutes Cooking 20 minutes

This is a dish traditional to Campania, in the south of Italy. There they use slow cooking to make tough cuts of meat tender. The tasty cooking liquid is saved to make a thick sauce to dress pasta at another meal. Here the meat is first made thin by beating, so it cooks quite quickly, and the sauce makes a delicious accompaniment.

60g/2oz capers, rinsed
60g/2oz sultanas
30g/1oz pine nuts
100g/3½oz prosciutto, finely chopped
3 tbsp white breadcrumbs
6 pork escalopes
salt and pepper
3 tbsp olive oil
3 tbsp dry white wine
200g/7oz can of chopped tomatoes
8 basil leaves, roughly torn

① Chop the capers, sultanas and nuts, then mix them together with the prosciutto and breadcrumbs.
② Put the pork between 2 layers of film and beat with a rolling pin to a thickness of about 5 mm/¼ inch. Season the pork, then spread some of the caper mixture over each slice and roll up tightly. Fasten with a toothpick or tie a little fine string around each roll.
③ Heat the oil in a frying pan and gently brown the pork rolls all over.
④ Add the wine, tomatoes and basil. Stir to scrape up any bits from the bottom of the pan, cover and cook gently for 15–20 minutes until the pork is tender.
⑤ Remove the toothpicks or string and serve the rolls with the sauce.

pan-seared pork stroganoff with porcini pasta twists

Preparation 10 minutes Cooking 20 minutes

Many larger supermarkets sell a selection of flavoured pastas – spinach, poppy seed, squid ink and basil. This dish is based around a pasta flavoured with porcini mushrooms, but it will work almost as well with plain pasta.

150g/5½oz porcini mushroom pasta
salt and pepper
2 tbsp olive oil
4 pork loin steaks
225g/8oz chestnut mushrooms,
  thickly sliced
2 garlic cloves, crushed
1 tsp fresh thyme leaves or
  ½ tsp dried
400ml/14fl oz carton of crème fraîche
4 tbsp chicken stock or white wine

1 Cook the pasta in boiling salted water for 20 minutes, or until *al dente*.
2 Meanwhile, heat the oil in a large pan and sear the pork on both sides for 2–3 minutes until golden. Remove from the pan and set aside.
3 Add the mushrooms and garlic to the pan and fry until they start to turn golden. Stir in the thyme, crème fraîche, stock or wine and salt and pepper to taste, then simmer gently until reduced to a sauce-like consistency.
4 Return the pork steaks to the pan and heat through.
5 Drain the pasta and spoon on to serving plates. Set a pork steak on each and spoon over the sauce.

minted lamb with couscous

115g/4oz couscous
1 red pepper, deseeded and thinly
  sliced
1 tbsp currants
275 ml/9½fl oz hot vegetable stock
4 lamb chump chops or leg steaks
salt and pepper
2 tbsp olive oil
2 garlic cloves, peeled
3 tbsp chopped mint
handful of toasted flaked almonds
juice of 1 lemon

1 Put the couscous in a heatproof bowl and stir in the pepper slices and currants. Pour over the hot stock and leave for 10 minutes – the couscous will soak up all the stock.

2 Meanwhile, sprinkle the lamb with salt and pepper. Heat the olive oil in a large frying pan and drop in the whole garlic cloves. Cook over a gentle heat for 30 seconds, then add the lamb. Cook for 3–4 minutes on each side until nicely browned. Remove and discard the garlic, then sprinkle the mint over the meat.

3 Fluff up the couscous with a spoon. Mix in the toasted almonds and season to taste.

4 Spoon the couscous on 4 serving plates and top with the lamb.

5 Heat the lemon juice in the frying pan with the pan juices. Bubble briefly, season, then pour over each serving.

Variation
You could also try this dish using boneless chicken breasts instead of the lamb, and thyme leaves instead of mint. (Depending on the size, they may need a slightly longer cooking time.)

lemon barbecued lamb with haricot mash   Serves 6

6 pieces of lamb neck fillet,
  each about 175g/6oz
1½ lemons, plus lemon wedges
  to serve
3 garlic cloves
4½ tsp ground cumin
salt and pepper
5 tbsp extra-virgin olive oil,
  plus more for drizzling
three 400g/14oz cans of haricot
  beans, drained

1 If barbecuing, light the barbecue about 45 minutes in advance. Cut the fillets almost in half horizontally, then open them out to make bigger flat pieces. Finely grate the zest from the lemons; squeeze and reserve the juice. Finely chop the garlic.

2 Mix the lemon rind with one-third of the cumin, half the garlic, and some salt and pepper. Put the opened-out lamb in a shallow dish and rub the rind mixture all over. Drizzle over 2 tablespoons of olive oil and rub in.

3 Process the beans to a purée in a food processor. Add the remaining olive oil, cumin, garlic and lemon juice, with salt and pepper to taste. Tip into a bowl.

4 Barbecue the lamb or cook on a preheated hot griddle pan for 3–4 minutes on each side, until charred on the outside and pink in the centre. If using a griddle, you may have to do this in batches; keep the cooked lamb on a warmed plate covered with foil in a low oven while you cook the rest.

5 While the lamb is cooking, warm the haricot purée through in the microwave for 3–4 minutes on High, or gently heat in a non-stick pan, stirring all the time.

6 Spoon the haricot mash on to each of 6 warmed plates and top with a piece of lamb. Drizzle over a little more oil and serve with lemon wedges.

tomato and olive chicken

Preparation 10 minutes Cooking about 30 minutes

Choose milder-flavoured olives, as strong ones can overpower the sauce. Try Greek Kalamata olives in jars or loose from the deli counter.

4 skinless chicken breast fillets,
  each about 140g/5oz
flour, for dusting
salt and pepper
2 tbsp olive oil
2 garlic cloves, chopped
2 tbsp sun-dried tomato paste
284ml/10fl oz tub of fresh chicken
  stock or 300ml/½ pint made from
  a (low-salt) cube
handful of black olives

1 Sprinkle the chicken breasts with a light dusting of flour, salt and pepper. Heat the olive oil in a large frying pan, add the chicken and fry on both sides until nicely browned and slightly crusty; about 10 minutes. Remove the chicken from the pan.

2 Add the garlic to the pan and fry briefly, then stir in the tomato paste, stock and some pepper. Bring to the boil, scraping the base of the pan to release the crusty bits, then return the chicken to the pan.

3 Add the olives, then simmer the chicken in the sauce for about 15 minutes, turning the breasts over halfway through, until the chicken is cooked through and the sauce is slightly thickened. Taste and add more salt if necessary – bear in mind that stock and olives can be salty so you may not need to add any more.

Variations
Thick cod or haddock steaks also work well with this treatment. Reduce the initial frying time to 5 minutes, then cook for a further 10 minutes.

chicken with prosciutto and fried sage leaves

Preparation 10 minutes Cooking 10 minutes

You can share the cooking of this dish – one of you can look after the chicken, while the other cooks the pasta. Toss the pasta with a little olive oil and freshly ground black pepper.

4 skinless chicken breast fillets
8 slices of prosciutto
2 tbsp plain flour
salt and pepper
2 tbsp olive oil
a good handful of sage leaves
60g/2oz butter
300ml/½ pint dry white wine
125ml/4fl oz double cream or
  crème fraîche
cooked pasta, to serve

① Put each chicken breast between 2 sheets of greaseproof paper and beat with a rolling pin until roughly twice its original size. Lay 2 rippled slices of prosciutto on top of each breast and secure with a cocktail stick. Dust each breast lightly with flour, season with salt and pepper and set aside.
② Heat the oil in a frying pan and fry the sage leaves for about 30 seconds until just crisp. Remove and drain on kitchen paper.
③ Add the butter to the pan and fry the chicken for 3–4 minutes on each side until well browned. (You may have to do this in batches or in 2 pans.)
④ Remove the chicken from the pan and set aside. Add the wine, stirring well to scrape all the bits from the bottom. Let the mixture bubble until the wine is reduced by about half.
⑤ Stir in the cream or crème fraîche, return the chicken to the pan and heat through.
⑥ Scatter in the fried sage leaves and serve with the pasta.

duck casserole with herbed new potatoes

Preparation 15 minutes Cooking 1¾ hours

Redcurrant jelly and mint give a lovely flavour to this non-fatty casserole. Slow cooking means the duck literally falls off the bone when you cut it.

4 duck legs, each about 300g/10oz
2 tbsp flour
salt and pepper
1 tbsp olive oil
1 large onion, thinly sliced
2 garlic cloves, finely chopped
1 tbsp finely chopped fresh rosemary
300ml/½ pint dry white wine
300ml/½ pint hot chicken stock
500g/1lb 2oz baby new potatoes,
   halved if large
200g/8oz frozen peas
2 tbsp redcurrant jelly
4 tbsp chopped fresh mint

1 Preheat the oven to 180°C/350°F/Gas 4. Dust the duck legs with the seasoned flour. Heat the olive oil in a wide, shallow flameproof casserole dish or large roasting tin, then fry the duck legs until well browned all over. Transfer to a plate.

2 Add the onion, garlic and rosemary to the dish or tin and cook for about 5 minutes, stirring frequently, until browned. Drain off any excess fat.

3 Return the duck legs to the dish or tin, then pour in the wine and bubble rapidly for 5 minutes. Add the stock and new potatoes.

4 If using a casserole dish, cover with a lid; if using a roasting tin, cover with a double thickness of foil, tightly sealed all round. Cook in the oven for 1½ hours.

5 Transfer the dish to the hob. Add the peas and redcurrant jelly and cook for 5 minutes, stirring occasionally, until the jelly has melted. Season with salt and pepper to taste and stir in the chopped mint.

spiced seville duck

Serves 6

Preparation 15 minutes Cooking 15 minutes

Remember to allow 2 hours for marinating the duck. If you can find them, do try to use Seville oranges for this dish, as their aromatic rind gives this dish a really incomparable flavour.

1½ tsp coriander seeds
18 black peppercorns
1 tsp ground cinnamon
pinch of freshly grated nutmeg
finely grated zest of 1 large orange,
   preferably Seville, and the juice of
   3 oranges (150 ml/1¼ pints)
6 duck breasts
1–2 mild chillies, deseeded and
   chopped
250ml/9fl oz chicken stock
3 tbsp redcurrant jelly
salt and pepper

1 Grind the spices to a fine powder using a pestle and mortar or coffee grinder. Stir in the orange zest.

2 Score the duck skin on each breast across at regular intervals just through to the flesh. Turn and score again to form a diamond pattern. Rub the spice mixture into the skin. Put the breasts, skin-side up, in a dish and leave to marinate in the fridge for at least 2 hours, or overnight.

3 Heat a non-stick frying pan until hot. Add the duck breasts, skin-side down and cook for 4–5 minutes until golden. Turn, lower the heat and cook for 5–6 minutes more, until cooked through (duck breast is best if still slightly pink). Remove from the pan, cover and keep warm.

4 Pour off all but about 1 tablespoon of fat from the pan. Add the chilli and cook gently until soft. Add the orange juice and stock, bring to the boil and boil rapidly for about 3–5 minutes until reduced by about half. Stir in the redcurrant jelly, together with any juices that have come from the cooked duck. Season to taste.

5 Serve the duck breasts with the sauce.

italian cod and garlic tomatoes

Preparation 15 minutes Cooking 40 minutes

Fish lovers, too, can tuck into a roast which also looks spectacular when it comes to the table. Choose a plump, firm-fleshed fish, such as cod or monkfish. The prosciutto provides contrast in flavour and colour. In summer, the fish can be stuffed and wrapped up to 1 hour ahead, then chilled.

2 unpeeled garlic cloves
3 tbsp olive oil
100g/4oz black olives
900g/2lb tomatoes
2 medium red chillies, deseeded
   and roughly chopped
salt and pepper
3 tbsp fresh pesto sauce
2 boneless skinless cod fillets,
   each about 450g/1lb
finely grated zest of 1 small lemon
12 slices of prosciutto

1 Preheat the oven to 200°C/400°F/Gas 6. Put the garlic in a roasting tin with 2 tablespoons of the oil and roast for 15 minutes, then remove from the oven. Add the olives, tomatoes and chillies to the tin and stir. Season well.

2 Spread the pesto over one side of a cod fillet and sprinkle over the lemon; season. Lay the other cod fillet on top, then wrap prosciutto slices loosely around the fish, tucking in the edges. Season with salt and drizzle over the remaining oil.

3 Put the cod on a rack over the roasting tin. Roast for 20 minutes until the fish is cooked and the tomatoes are starting to break up.

4 Transfer the cod to a plate. Mash the garlic into the pan juices and discard the skins; season. Slice the cod and serve with the olives, tomatoes and pan juices.

fish salad with lemon basil dressing

Serves 6 as a main-course salad

Preparation 15 minutes

These delicate summery flavours are perfect for a leisurely lunch. Just serve with some warm herb bread and chilled white wine. If you have a chance, marinate the salmon for up to 1 hour in the fridge.

400g/14oz large cooked peeled prawns
200g/8oz smoked salmon, sliced
juice of 1 large lemon (4 tbsp) plus
   2 tsp finely grated zest
generous handful of basil leaves
2 tbsp chopped fresh parsley
salt and pepper
120g/4¼oz bag of mixed salad leaves
4 spring onions
½ cucumber
250g/9oz cherry tomatoes

for the lemon basil dressing
5 tbsp light olive oil
juice of 1 large lemon (4 tbsp) plus
   1 tsp finely grated zest
generous handful of basil leaves

1 Put the prawns and salmon in a shallow dish. Add the juice of 1 of the lemons with 2 teaspoons of the lemon zest, together with half the basil and the parsley; season. Toss together and leave to marinate while you prepare the rest of the salad.

2 Make the dressing: mix together all the ingredients and season.

3 Tip the mixed salad leaves into a bowl. Slice the spring onions at an angle. Cut the cucumber into long thin strips, preferably using a mandoline grater. Add the cucumber, onions and tomatoes to the salad, then toss together with the dressing.

4 To serve, put a pile of the salad on each plate and top with the marinated salmon and prawns.

black bean roasted sea bass with ginger

Preparation 10 minutes Cooking 10–15 minutes

This is a popular dish in Japanese and Chinese cooking. Sandwiching the fillets together before roasting them keeps the flesh moist.

3 sea bass, each about 450g/1lb
    (prepared weight), filleted but
    skin left on
2 tbsp groundnut oil
2 tsp black soy bean paste, such
    as miso
2.5cm/1 inch piece of fresh root
    ginger, peeled and finely shredded
3 spring onions, trimmed and finely
    shredded lengthwise
salt and pepper
1 tbsp sesame oil
350g/12oz mange-tout peas
1 tbsp salted black soy beans in
    brine, drained

1 Preheat oven to 250°C/475°F/Gas 9. Cut each fillet across into halves. Heat 1 tablespoon of the groundnut oil in a frying pan and sear the fish, skin side down, for about 30 seconds, then lay skin side up on a chopping board.

2 Smear a thin layer of black bean paste across the skin of each fillet. Turn half of the fillets skin side down and scatter with ginger and spring onions; season. Sandwich, flesh to flesh, with the remaining fillets. Put on a baking sheet, brush with sesame oil and roast for 5 minutes.

3 Meanwhile, heat the remaining groundnut oil with a dash of sesame oil and stir-fry the mange-tout and soy beans; season.

4 Serve each portion of sea bass in a shallow bowl on a bed of mange-tout with the black beans.

pan-fried red mullet fillets with chilli ginger dressing

Preparation 10 minutes Cooking 7–8 minutes

To give the fish a lovely crispy skin, make sure the oil is good and hot before adding the fillets. Also, use a large pan so the fillets have a chance to cook evenly in one layer.

1 tbsp flour
salt and pepper
8 red mullet or tilapia fillets, skin on
4 tbsp olive oil
350g/12oz spinach, stems removed
5cm/2 inch piece of fresh root
    ginger, peeled and cut into very
    thin slivers
1 fresh medium-hot green chilli,
    deseeded and cut into very thin
    slivers
juice of 1 lime
6 spring onions, cut into thin strips
2–3 tsp toasted sesame seeds,
    to serve

1 Season the flour with salt and pepper on a plate, then coat the fish in it. Heat 2 tablespoons of the oil in a large non-stick frying pan and fry the fillets, skin-side down, for 2–3 minutes, until the skin is crisp. (If you don't have a large enough pan, do it in 2 pans or cook in batches.) Turn and fry for 2 minutes more or until cooked through. Remove and keep warm.

2 Add the spinach to the pan and stir just until it wilts. (It will cook in the water that clings to the leaves after it is washed and will be done in no more than 30 seconds.) Press lightly in a sieve or colander to remove excess water. Keep warm.

3 Wipe the pan, add the remaining oil and heat. Add the ginger and the chilli and fry for about 1 minute until softened. Stir in the lime juice to taste. Remove from the heat and stir in the spring onions. The warmth from the pan should heat them through, softening them very slightly.

4 Divide the spinach between 4 warm plates. Top each with 2 fish fillets, skin-side up, and season with salt and pepper. Pile the ginger and chilli on top, then spoon the dressing over and around the fish. Sprinkle with sesame seeds.

salmon with tarragon cream sauce

Preparation 5 minutes Cooking about 20 minutes

4 salmon fillets

salt and pepper

2 tbsp vegetable oil

2 shallots or 1 small onion, finely
  chopped

4 tbsp chopped fresh tarragon

175ml/6fl oz whipping cream

3 tbsp chopped fresh parsley

lemon wedges, to serve

new potatoes and green beans,
  to serve

1 Preheat the oven to 180°C/350°F/Gas 4. Season the salmon steaks on both sides with salt and pepper. Heat the oil in a frying pan (preferably non-stick) until fairly hot. Add the salmon, flesh-side down, and fry quickly for about 3 minutes until lightly browned. Turn over and fry the skin side for 2 minutes.

2 Transfer to a shallow ovenproof dish big enough just to take the fish in a single layer and sprinkle over the shallot or onion and the tarragon. Spoon over the cream and some seasoning.

3 Cook in the oven for 12–15 minutes, until the salmon is cooked.

4 Sprinkle with chopped parsley, transfer to warm plates and garnish with lemon wedges. Serve with new potatoes and green beans.

griddled salmon with lime and chilli butter

Preparation 5 minutes Cooking 8 minutes

Flavoured butters are a boon for the busy cook. You can make them in bulk ahead of time, roll them in foil and chill or freeze, and then cut off discs as and when you need them. A pat of garlic-and-parsley butter makes a plain steak into *haute cuisine*; blue cheese butter does almost the same for a burger, and lemon-and-tarragon butter lifts a simple grilled chicken breast.

50g/2oz butter, softened

4 salmon fillets, each about 200g/8oz

½ tsp chilli powder

salt and pepper

finely grated zest and juice of 1 lime

2 tbsp chopped fresh coriander

lime wedges, to serve

green salad and new potatoes,
  to serve

1 Light a barbecue well ahead or preheat the grill or a heavy griddle pan. Smear a little of the butter over the skin of each salmon fillet and season with a little of the chilli powder and some salt and pepper. Drizzle over a little of the lime juice.

2 Cook the fish for 8 minutes, turning the fillets halfway through.

3 Meanwhile, mix together the remaining butter and chilli powder with the lime zest and remaining juice, and the coriander. Season well with salt and pepper.

4 When the salmon fillets are cooked, put one on each serving plate and top with generous knobs of the lime and chilli butter. Serve hot with lime wedges, a green salad and new potatoes.

Variations
You could also flavour the butter with crushed garlic and snipped fresh chives, or Dijon mustard and chopped fresh parsley or basil.

Few things are as useful to those with guests to feed and no time as **salmon fillets**. As well as cooking quickly, whether it be by frying, grilling or baking, their rich moist flesh suits a myriad of flavourings and treatments. Strangely enough, too, despite the fact that salmon is now generally cheaper than more homely fish like **cod**, it still manages to convey a sense of occasion. If you really want your guests to feel honoured, of course, it is well worth the expense of getting some wild salmon for its wonderful full flavour.

The secret of success: as with most fish, when cooking salmon take care not to overcook it as the flesh will then dry up unappetisingly, particularly that of tender fillets.

Flavours that go well with salmon: salmon fillets take flavour well in marinating, or you can coat them with a crust or bake them *en papillote* with some aromatic flavourings. Suitable candidates run the gamut from the **subtle**, like the herb coating that follows, to the **spicy** and **citrus-sharp**, as with our Moroccan treatment. You could also try lime juice and crushed mixed peppercorns, olives and crumbled chèvre, or cucumber and crème fraîche.

Spring Herb Salmon with Warm Tomato Dressing couldn't be simpler but delivers a wonderfully fresh result. Brush some salmon fillets with oil and season. Mix a good large handful of roughly torn **fresh herbs**, like dill, chervil, tarragon and parsley, and press on top of the fillets. Heat some **oil** in a frying pan and cook the salmon, herb-side down, for about 2 minutes over a high heat until golden. Turn, lower the heat and cook for 4–5 minutes, until just cooked through (the flesh flakes when forked). Set aside in a warm place. Deseed a couple of tasty **tomatoes** and chop the flesh finely. Toss into the pan and cook briefly until the juices start to run. Add the juice of a **lemon** and season well. Serve the fish with the pan sauce and some boiled **asparagus** and **potatoes**.

Baked Salmon with Preserved Lemon Chermoula uses Moroccan *chermoula* marinade. In a shallow dish large enough to take the salmon in one layer, mix some finely chopped garlic, ¼ preserved lemon (available from better food shops), 4 tablespoons each chopped coriander and flat-leaf parsley, a pinch of saffron, ½ teaspoon paprika, ¼ teaspoon cayenne, 2 tablespoons each olive oil, lemon juice and water. Coat 4 skinned salmon fillets with this marinade, rubbing in well. Cover and leave in a cool place for at least 2 hours. Cut 4 rectangles of foil large enough to hold the fish comfortably and lay shiny side down. Put a fillet in the centre of each and spoon over the marinade. Top with a knob of butter and a pinch of crushed chillies. Season. Fold the foil over the fish and seal to make parcels. Bake in an oven preheated to 220°C/425°F/Gas 7 for 20 minutes. Serve garnished with black olives.

plaice goujons in a tea batter

Preparation 15 minutes Cooking 10 minutes

Although it sounds unusual, tea makes a brilliant light batter with a fine flavour.

100g/4oz self-raising flour, plus more
 for coating
salt and pepper
225ml/8fl oz cold tea, such as Assam
4 plaice fillets, about 600g/1¾lb total
 weight, skinned and cut into strips
groundnut or sunflower oil, for frying
lemon or lime wedges, to serve

for the dipping sauce
100ml/3½fl oz white wine vinegar
85g/3oz caster sugar
1 red chilli, halved deseeded and
 finely chopped
5cm/2 inch piece of cucumber,
 quartered lengthwise and thinly
 sliced

1. Put the flour in a bowl with a pinch of salt. Make a well in the centre and gradually beat in the tea to make a thin batter that just coats the back of a wooden spoon. It should be about the same consistency as unwhipped single cream.
2. Make the dipping sauce: put the vinegar and the sugar in a small pan and heat gently, stirring all the time, until the sugar dissolves. Increase the heat and boil for about 3–4 minutes until it forms a light syrup. Remove from the heat and stir in the chilli and cucumber. Spoon into 4 small dishes.
3. Toss the plaice strips lightly in seasoned flour. Heat 2.5cm/1 inch of oil in a wide pan or wok. Dip the plaice in the batter, then fry for 3 minutes or until crisp and golden (you may need to do this in batches).
4. Sprinkle with sea salt and serve with the sauce and lemon or lime wedges, and chips if you like.

grilled trout with cashew and garlic butter

Preparation 5 minutes Cooking about 12 minutes

4 whole trout, each about 200g/7oz
vegetable oil, for brushing
salt and pepper
50g/2oz butter
50g/2oz shelled cashew nuts
2 garlic cloves, finely chopped
good handful of chopped parsley
juice of 1 lemon
boiled new potatoes, to serve

1. Preheat a hot grill or barbecue. Slash the skins of the fish deeply three times along each side to let the heat permeate the flesh. Remove the heads if you like. Brush the fish lightly with oil and season with salt and pepper, both inside and out.
2. Cook under the preheated grill or on the barbecue for about 4 minutes on each side, until the skin is browned and the flesh feels firm. (Or spear with the tip of a knife – the flesh should look flaky.)
3. Melt the butter in a wide shallow pan, and fry the nuts quickly until toasted. Add the garlic and parsley, and fry the mixture briefly until the parsley darkens slightly.
4. Add the lemon juice with more salt and pepper to taste and heat through.
5. Put each trout on a warmed serving plate, spoon over the cashew and garlic butter, and serve with boiled new potatoes.

pak choi and carrot rösti

Preparation 15 minutes Cooking 20 minutes

200ml/7fl oz crème fraîche
1 tsp Dijon mustard
salt and pepper
1 small onion, thinly sliced
450g/1lb potatoes, coarsely grated
2 carrots, coarsely grated
2 tbsp chopped fresh flat-leaf
  parsley
2 tsp black mustard seeds, plus
  more to serve (optional)
3 tbsp olive oil
2 garlic cloves, crushed
200g/7oz pak choi, halved lengthwise

1 In a small bowl, mix together the crème fraîche and the mustard and season to taste. Chill until ready to use.

2 In a large bowl, mix together the onion, potato, carrot, parsley and mustard seeds. Divide the mixture into 8 equal portions. Heat 1 tablespoon of the olive oil in a large frying pan and add 4 portions of the mixture, spaced well apart, then flatten them with a fish slice. Fry for 4–5 minutes on each side until golden. Keep hot. Heat another tablespoon of the oil in the pan and fry the remaining mixture in the same way.

3 Meanwhile, in a wok or large frying pan, heat the remaining olive oil and gently fry the garlic for 1–2 minutes. Add the pak choi and toss together until lightly wilted. Season well.

4 Place 2 rösti on each of 4 warmed plates and top with the garlic greens and some crème fraîche. Sprinkle with extra black mustard seeds if you like.

rustic noodles with cabbage, anchovies and melted cheese

Preparation 15 minutes Cooking about 20 minutes

Soba noodles are a traditional Japanese pasta made from buckwheat. If you don't spot them with the Italian pasta in your supermarket, try the Oriental section or use Italian buckwheat pasta instead.

280g/10oz potatoes, diced
salt and pepper
175g/6oz soba (or Italian buckwheat)
  noodles
3 tbsp olive oil
2 red onions, cut into wedges
3 garlic cloves, chopped
225g/8oz Savoy cabbage, shredded
250g/9oz tub of mascarpone cheese
250g/9oz packet of Taleggio or
  Fontina cheese, rind removed and
  cut into dice
50g/1¾oz can of anchovy fillets,
  drained and halved lengthwise

1 Cook the potatoes in a pan of boiling salted water for 5 minutes. Add the noodles and cook for 5 minutes more until the noodles are just *al dente*.

2 Meanwhile, heat the oil in a large, deep frying pan and fry the onions and garlic until softening and starting to colour. Add the cabbage, then cover and cook for 3–5 minutes, until the cabbage is just tender.

3 Thoroughly drain the potatoes and noodles, then add to the onions and cabbage with some pepper and toss until well mixed.

4 Spoon in the mascarpone and scatter over the Taleggio or Fontina and the anchovies. Heat until the cheese melts to a creamy sauce and serve immediately.

Variation
If you're not too fond of anchovies, replace them with a couple of chopped rashers of crispy smoked bacon.

goats' cheese and thyme soufflés

Serves 2 (easily doubled)

Preparation 15 minutes Cooking 10–12 minutes

This inventive way of serving a soufflé is a creation of Alice Waters of the restaurant Chez Panisse in California. The version here, by London chef and restaurateur Sally Clarke, doesn't take long to cook and eliminates the need to make a traditional sauce base. If the egg whites are at room temperature, they will give you more volume.

knob of unsalted butter, melted

50g/2oz Parmesan cheese, finely grated

2 eggs, separated

100g/4oz soft goats' cheese

3 tbsp double cream

½ tsp chopped fresh thyme, plus thyme leaves, to garnish

salt and pepper

1 Put a baking sheet in the oven and preheat to 200°C/400°F/Gas 6. Using a pastry brush, grease the insides of 2 shallow ovenproof soup plates with the melted butter and sprinkle them with a quarter of the Parmesan. Shake off any excess.

2 In a bowl, whisk the egg yolks until smooth, then add the goats' cheese and whisk again. Stir in the cream and the chopped thyme, and season. Fold in half the remaining Parmesan.

3 In another bowl, whisk the egg whites with a pinch of salt to stiff peaks.

4 Fold the egg whites carefully but thoroughly into the cheese mixture, divide between the soup plates and sprinkle with the thyme leaves and remaining Parmesan.

5 Put the soufflés on the baking sheet and bake for 10–12 minutes, until risen and golden. Serve immediately.

soft polenta with pak choi and soy dressing

Preparation 10 minutes Cooking 15 minutes

The Italians serve soft polenta much like we serve mashed potatoes – to soak up delicious sauces and gravies. As an alternative, you could pour the mixture into a shallow tin then cool it until firm and set. Cut it into slices, grill until golden and serve with the vegetable mixture piled on top.

1.4 litres/2½ pints vegetable stock

250g/9oz quick-cook polenta

1 tbsp Thai seven-spice paste

1 tbsp chilli sauce

1 tbsp soy sauce

1 tsp finely chopped garlic

1 tsp finely chopped ginger

1 tbsp sesame oil

1 red chilli, thinly sliced

115g/4oz shiitake mushrooms, halved

4 heads of pak choi, halved lengthwise

1 Pour the stock into a large pan and bring to a rolling boil. Shower in the polenta, stirring constantly. Stir in the Thai spice paste and simmer over a low heat for 4–5 minutes, stirring. Season to taste.

2 Meanwhile, in a small bowl, mix together the chilli sauce, soy sauce, garlic and ginger and 2 tablespoons water.

3 Heat the sesame oil in a larger frying pan or wok and stir-fry the sliced chilli and mushrooms for 1 minute. Add the pak choi and 4 tablespoons water and stir-fry until the water has evaporated. Pour over the soy sauce mixture and bring to the boil.

4 Divide the polenta between 4 shallow serving bowls and top with the stir-fried vegetables and soy dressing.

indian chickpea salad

Preparation 15 minutes Cooking 15 minutes

6 tbsp olive oil
3 garlic cloves, sliced
2 red chillies, halved, deseeded
   and sliced
4 tsp cumin seeds, lightly crushed
two 400g/14oz cans of chickpeas,
   drained and rinsed
3 tomatoes, halved, deseeded
   and diced
pared rind and juice of 1 lemon
salt and pepper
1 naan bread

for the salad
30g/1oz fresh coriander leaves
½ cucumber, cut into thick batons
1 medium red onion, thinly sliced
125g/4½oz fresh baby spinach

to serve (optional)
Greek-style yoghurt
chopped fresh mint

1 Put 5 tablespoons of the oil into a large pan and add the garlic, chillies and cumin. Warm over a medium heat for 10 minutes, taking care that the garlic doesn't burn. Meanwhile, preheat the grill to high.

2 Add the chickpeas and warm through for 5 minutes.

3 Add the tomatoes, lemon rind and juice to the chickpeas and season. Set aside.

4 Brush the naan with the remaining oil. Grill both sides until crisp and golden, then tear into 3cm/1¼ inch pieces.

5 Toss the salad ingredients together with salt and pepper to taste.

6 Divide the salad between 4 plates, spoon the chickpea mixture over and top with the naan croutons. Serve with Greek-style yoghurt flavoured with fresh mint, if you like.

When time is short, invariably the last course is sacrificed. This needn't be the case, however, even when you're not entertaining. There are lots of delicious quick desserts that make the most of healthy seasonal fruit or simple store-cupboard staples. If all else fails, there's always ice cream, and there are lots of ideas for serving it with a flourish.

dashing desserts

chocolate baked ricotta

Preparation 5 minutes Cooking 25 minutes

This rich baked chocolate-cheesecake-style pudding is flavoured with cinnamon and served with soft poached tamarillos. If you can't find these tart but tasty South American fruits, this dessert is almost as superb with poached plums. Don't forget to allow time for the tamarillos to cool completely.

oil, for greasing
250g/9oz plain chocolate
500g/1lb 2oz ricotta cheese
whites of 2 medium eggs, lightly
 beaten
1 tsp ground cinnamon
300ml/½ pint whipping cream,
 whipped, to serve
cocoa powder, to dust

for the poached tamarillos
100g/3½oz caster sugar
300ml/½ pint sweet white wine
1 vanilla pod, split
6 ripe tamarillos

1 Preheat the oven to 200°C/400°F/Gas 6. Oil the base and sides of a 25x11x8cm/10x4½x3¼ inch loaf tin and line with greaseproof paper.

2 Poach the tamarillos: place the sugar, wine, vanilla pod and 150 ml/¼ pint water in a large pan and stir over a low heat until the sugar has completely dissolved. Slit the tamarillos down the middle, taking care not to cut all the way through to the stalk. Add to the wine syrup, bring to the boil and simmer for 5 minutes until just tender. Leave to cool completely.

3 Meanwhile, melt the chocolate in a bowl set over a pan of simmering water, making sure that the bottom of the bowl doesn't touch the water. Remove from the heat and allow to cool slightly.

4 In a large bowl, beat together the ricotta, melted chocolate, egg whites and cinnamon until well combined. Spoon into the prepared tin and level the surface with the back of a wet spoon.

5 Bake for 25 minutes until firm to the touch. Allow to cool completely. Turn out and remove the greaseproof paper.

6 Serve cut into fingers and topped with the whipped cream and poached fruit. Dust lightly with cocoa to serve.

chocolate baskets with berries

Preparation 10 minutes

450g/1lb mixed blueberries and
 raspberries, thawed if frozen
4 tbsp honey or icing sugar
125ml/4fl oz crème fraîche
2 tbsp brandy, whisky, amaretto
 or Grand Marnier (optional)
4 ready-made plain chocolate cases
4 sprigs of fresh mint (optional),
 to decorate
cocoa powder and icing sugar,
 for dusting

1 Reserve about one-third of the fruit for decoration, then liquidize or process the rest. Press through a sieve and sweeten with 2 tablespoons of the honey or icing sugar.

2 Mix the crème fraîche with the remaining honey or sugar and alcohol, if using, then spoon into the chocolate cases.

3 Spoon half the sauce on to each plate, add the chocolate cases and decorate with the reserved berries and sprigs of mint, if using.

4 Dust with cocoa and icing sugar to serve.

velvet chocolate torte

Preparation 15 minutes, plus 4 hours' chilling

12 Hobnob (or other oaty) biscuits
50g/2oz butter, melted
whites of 2 eggs
85g/3oz caster sugar
250g/9oz plain chocolate
284ml/10fl oz carton of double cream
2 tbsp brandy
sifted icing sugar, to decorate
single cream, to serve

1 In a large, strong plastic food bag, crush the biscuits to crumbs with a rolling pin. Stir into the butter until evenly mixed. Set aside 2 tablespoons of the crumb mixture, then press the rest over the base of a 20cm/8 inch loose-bottomed cake tin and smooth down with the back of a large metal spoon. Chill the base while you make the filling.

2 In a mixing bowl set over a pan of simmering water, whisk the egg whites with the sugar for about 5 minutes until they form a stiff meringue that stands in soft peaks.

3 Break up the chocolate and melt in the microwave on Medium for 3–4 minutes or in a small bowl set over the pan of hot water left over from making the meringue. Whip the cream until it just holds its shape.

4 Fold the chocolate into the meringue, followed by the cream and the brandy. Pour into the tin and smooth the top. Sprinkle with the reserved crumbs and chill for at least 4 hours, or preferably overnight, so it is softly set.

5 Just before serving, remove the torte from the tin, slide on to a plate and dust lightly with icing sugar. Cut into wedges with a warm knife and serve with cream.

croissant and chocolate pudding

Serves 6

Preparation 10 minutes Cooking 30–35 minutes

This is a scrumptious chocolate version of bread and butter pudding, with the texture of brown velvet.

85g/3oz butter, plus more for
  the dish
4 croissants
115g/4oz good-quality plain
  chocolate, broken into pieces
142ml/5fl oz carton of cream
300ml/½ pint milk
4 tbsp dark rum or brandy
115g/4oz caster sugar
pinch of ground cinnamon
3 eggs
icing sugar, for dusting
single cream, to serve

1 Preheat the oven to 180°C/350°F/Gas 4. Lightly butter a 1.25litre/2 pint gratin dish. Cut the croissants into strips with scissors. In a bowl set over a pan of simmering water, heat the chocolate, cream, milk, rum or

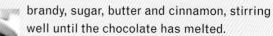

brandy, sugar, butter and cinnamon, stirring well until the chocolate has melted.

2 In a separate bowl, whisk the eggs, then pour the chocolate mixture into them, whisking constantly until everything is well mixed.

3 Arrange the croissant strips haphazardly in the gratin dish. Pour the chocolate mixture evenly over the croissants, press them down with a fork and leave to stand for 10 minutes before baking.

4 Bake the pudding for 30–35 minutes, until the top is crunchy and the inside is soft and squidgy. Leave to stand for 10 minutes before serving.

5 Dust with icing sugar and serve with cream.

ten-minute tiramisu

Preparation 10 minutes

This is so much better if made using proper fresh coffee, preferably made in a cafetière, as it gives a fuller, richer flavour. If you don't have one, use a jug: put two heaped tablespoons of freshly ground coffee in a large heatproof measuring jug and pour over boiling water to come up to the 400ml/14fl oz mark. Stir everything well, cover and leave for 4 minutes. Strain through a tea strainer into another jug – you'll now have just the right amount of perfectly flavoured coffee for this recipe.

18 sponge finger biscuits
300ml/¼ pint hot black coffee
4 tbsp brandy
4 tbsp caster sugar
150ml/¼ pint double cream
500g/1lb 2oz tub of mascarpone
60g/2oz dark chocolate, coarsely
  grated

1 Break each sponge finger into three. Put nine pieces into each of six tumblers or glass dessert dishes.
2 Mix the coffee with the brandy and 1 tablespoon of the sugar, stirring until this has dissolved. Carefully drizzle the liquid evenly over the biscuits and leave to soak.
3 In a bowl, lightly whip the cream until it just holds its shape. In a separate bowl, beat the mascarpone with the remaining sugar, then fold in the cream.
4 Sprinkle half the chocolate over the biscuits, then top with dollops of the mascarpone cream. Sprinkle the remaining chocolate over the cream.
5 Serve immediately or chill for up to 4 hours before serving.

irish coffee sundaes

Preparation 5 minutes Cooking 5 minutes

This is one occasion when it is best to serve ice cream straight from the freezer. There is no need to give it a little time to soften as you are going to pour hot coffee over it. Depending on your ice cream, it can however be hard to scoop it straight from the freezer. Soft scoop is not suitable for this recipe, so if you get a chance, scoop the ice cream on to a chilled baking sheet ahead of time and return it to the freezer until ready to serve. We've used Irish whiskey because it has such lovely sweet maize and barley flavours. Use an unrefined demerara sugar, because it gives a superior, richer, more rounded flavour to the whiskey sauce.

two 500ml/18fl oz tubs of good-
  quality vanilla ice cream (you won't
  need it all)
300ml/½ pint very strong hot fresh
  coffee
4 tbsp Irish whiskey
1 tbsp demerara sugar
langues-de-chat or shortbread
  biscuits, to serve (optional)

1 Put two or three scoops of ice cream into each serving bowl, then simply mix together the coffee, whiskey and sugar and pour this over the ice cream.
2 Serve at once, with langues-de-chat or shortbread biscuits, if you like.

speedy rice pudding brûlées

Preparation 10 minutes Cooking 5 minutes

411g/14½oz can of peach slices
  in natural juice
¼ tsp ground cinnamon
finely grated zest of ½ orange
425g/15oz can of rice pudding
4 tbsp demerara sugar

❶ Preheat the grill to high. Drain the peaches and cut each peach slice into three pieces, then divide them between four 175ml/6fl oz ramekins or heatproof dishes. Sprinkle the cinnamon over the peaches.
❷ Stir the orange zest into the rice pudding, then spoon over the peaches. Smooth the tops with the back of a spoon, then sprinkle them evenly with the sugar.
❸ Grill for 5 minutes, until the sugar has caramelized.
❹ Allow to cool before serving.

cardamom spiced puddings

Preparation 10 minutes Cooking 15 minutes

4 cardamom pods
15g/½oz demerara sugar
60g/2oz flaked rice
600ml/1 pint semi-skimmed milk

for the topping
2 tbsp demerara sugar
2 tbsp shelled pistachio nuts,
  chopped

❶ Slit the cardamom pods with a sharp knife and scoop out the seeds. Grind together the seeds and sugar in a pestle and mortar, or grind in a sturdy bowl with the end of a rolling pin.
❷ Put the cardamom-scented sugar in a pan with the rice and milk. Bring to the boil, then lower the heat and simmer for 12-15 minutes, stirring occasionally, until cooked. Divide between 4 small heatproof dishes and leave for 5 minutes.
❸ Preheat the grill to high. Prepare the topping; sprinkle the puddings with the sugar and grill for 3-4 minutes, until bubbling-hot and glazed.
❹ Scatter with the pistachios and serve.

rhubarb and strawberry cream fool

Preparation 10 minutes Cooking 15 minutes

Don't forget to allow enough time for the cooked fruit to cool before adding the custard and cream.

450g/1lb rhubarb, cut into chunks
85g/3oz golden caster sugar
250g/9oz strawberries, hulled
half a 400g/14oz carton of ready-made custard
142ml/5fl oz carton of extra-thick double cream

1 Put the rhubarb and sugar in a pan and simmer, stirring often, for 10 minutes until pulpy.
2 Halve or quarter the strawberries, depending on size, stir into the rhubarb and cook for 5 minutes until softened. Remove from the heat and allow to cool.
3 When cold, set aside 4 tablespoons of the mixture. Beat the custard and cream into the remainder and spoon this into 4 glasses.
4 Swirl a tablespoon of the reserved mixture into the top of each glass.

strawberry crush

Preparation 10 minutes

200ml/7fl oz carton of crème fraîche
200g/7oz carton of Greek-style yoghurt
8 amaretti biscuits
225g/8oz strawberries, hulled and roughly chopped
1 tbsp icing sugar

1 Beat the crème fraîche and yoghurt together in a bowl.
2 Break the amaretti up into pieces and stir into the mixture.
3 Roughly mash the strawberries with icing sugar so you make a little juice, but the fruit stays in pieces.
4 Gently swirl the strawberries and sugar into the yoghurt mix and spoon this into 4 glasses.

Variations
To smarten up this dessert for midweek entertaining, pour a little cassis over the top before serving. It's also delicious made with 300ml/½ pint whipped cream instead of the yoghurt and crème fraîche, and crushed meringues instead of the amaretti.

summer berry brûlée

Preparation 10 minutes, plus few minutes' chilling

This is the perfect pud to round off a barbie, as it is refreshing and can be made several hours ahead. Make double quantities for a party.

450g/1lb strawberries
225g/8oz raspberries
2 tbsp caster sugar
grated zest and juice of 1 orange
200g/7oz tub of Greek-style yoghurt
200ml/7fl oz tub of crème fraîche
3 tbsp light muscovado sugar
a few pinches of ground cinnamon

❶ Hull and slice the strawberries and put in a non-metallic serving dish with the raspberries. Sprinkle over 1 tablespoon of the caster sugar and the grated orange zest and juice.
❷ Mix together the yoghurt, crème fraîche and remaining caster sugar, then spread this over the fruit to cover. Sprinkle over the muscovado sugar and cinnamon.
❸ Chill for a few minutes until the sugar turns syrupy.

Variations
When the strawberries finish, use sliced peaches, nectarines and loganberries or blackberries.

raspberry cream with crunchy caramelized oats

Preparation 10 minutes Cooking 3 minutes

Oats mixed with sugar can burn very quickly under a hot grill, so keep a constant watch and turn them occasionally for even browning, especially once the sugar starts to melt. Try to use jumbo rolled oats for extra crunch and don't forget to allow time for them to cool after toasting.

25g/1oz porridge oats
3 tbsp demerara sugar
¼ tsp ground cinnamon
250g/9oz fresh raspberries
142ml/5fl oz carton of extra-thick
  double cream
200g/7oz carton of Greek-style
  yoghurt

❶ Preheat the grill. Sprinkle the oats on a baking sheet. Mix in 2 tablespoons of the sugar and the cinnamon. Toast under the grill, turning often, until golden and the sugar is starting to melt, about 3 minutes. Set aside to cool. If the oats stick together, break them up with your fingers.
❷ Set aside two-thirds of the raspberries. In a bowl with a fork, crush the rest lightly with the remaining sugar so you just release some of their juices. Gently stir in most of the cooled oats, reserving about a spoonful of them for sprinkling over, and swirl in the cream and yoghurt.
❸ Spoon the mixture into 4 bowls, top with the reserved raspberries, then scatter over the reserved oats.

blackberry sherry creams

Preparation 5 minutes

With a total of only five ingredients, these little pots are a treat to make after you've come home from picking some blackberries.

142ml/5fl oz carton of thick double
  cream
250g/9oz tub of mascarpone cheese
3 tbsp sherry
2 tbsp caster sugar
about 200g/8oz fresh blackberries
icing sugar, for dusting

1 Beat together the cream, mascarpone, sherry and sugar until smooth.
2 Divide between 4 small dishes and smooth the tops.
3 Arrange a few blackberries on top of the desserts and lightly dust with icing sugar.

Variations
Instead of blackberries you could also use loganberries or tayberries. For a special dinner party dessert, drizzle a little fruit liqueur, such as cassis, over each cream just before serving.

apricot and ginger snap glory

Preparation 10 minutes

400g/14oz can of apricot halves
  in juice, drained
two 150g/5oz cartons of fat-free
  Greek-style yoghurt
2 tsp icing sugar
large pinch of ground cinnamon
4 ginger snap biscuits

1 Divide half the apricots between 4 large wine glasses.
2 Mix the yoghurt, icing sugar and cinnamon together. Spoon half the mixture on top of the apricots.
3 Seal the biscuits in a plastic bag and bash with a rolling pin to crush them roughly (but don't turn them into dust).
4 Sprinkle half the crumbs over the yoghurt, reserving the rest.
5 Arrange the rest of the apricots on top and spoon over the rest of the yoghurt mixture. Chill until ready.
6 Just before serving, sprinkle the rest of the crumbs on top of the yoghurt.

oranges in ginger caramel

The caramel is best poured over the oranges just before serving.

225g/8oz sugar
4 pieces of stem ginger, finely diced
4 oranges
half-fat crème fraîche, to serve

1 Put the sugar and 200ml/7fl oz water in a pan. Stir over a medium heat until the sugar has dissolved. Increase the heat and boil rapidly for about 10 minutes, without stirring, until the syrup is golden. Remove from heat and immediately pour in 3 tablespoons of cold water – the caramel may splutter. Allow to cool slightly, then stir in the stem ginger. Set aside.

2 Remove the skin and pith from the oranges with a sharp knife. Cut each orange horizontally into slices and arrange these, slightly overlapping, on 4 serving plates.

3 Spoon the ginger caramel over the oranges and serve with crème fraîche.

orange semi-freddo with orange sauce

Serves 6

The Italian *semi-freddo* (semi-frozen) is very refreshing to have on a warm summer evening. Serving ice cream this way means you get more intense flavours coming through.

4 eggs
175g/6oz caster sugar
finely grated zest of 4 large
  oranges, plus the juice from 2
600ml/1 pint double cream

for the sauce
3 oranges
85g/3oz caster sugar

1 Crack the eggs into a large heatproof bowl and tip in 150g/5oz of the sugar. Set over a pan of simmering water and whisk with a hand blender for 5 minutes until the mixture is pale and foamy. It should leave a trail on the surface when the whisks are lifted out. Whisk in the orange zest and juice.

2 In a separate bowl, whisk the cream with the remaining sugar until it just holds its shape. Carefully fold the cream into the egg mixture, taking care not to knock out too much of the air.

3 Pour the mixture into a rigid plastic container and freeze for 3–4 hours until it has just set.

4 Meanwhile, make the sauce: peel the rind from 1 orange, taking care not to remove any of the white pith. Thinly slice the peel into tiny strips and squeeze the juice from all the oranges. Put the sugar in a pan with 2 tablespoons of water and heat gently until dissolved. Add the orange juice and sliced peel. Bring to the boil and simmer for 10–12 minutes until syrupy and reduced by half. Pour into a jug and allow to cool.

5 Serve the semi-freddo with the orange sauce drizzled over it.

Variation
You can replace the orange zest and juice with 2 teaspoons of vanilla extract and 175g/6oz grated plain chocolate. Whisk them into the egg mixture at the end of step 1. Make a quick chocolate sauce by melting 100g/3½oz plain chocolate pieces with a 142ml/5fl oz tub of double cream over a gentle heat.

fruit tea jelly

Preparation 15 minutes

Use whatever fruit you fancy, but bear in mind the colour. Berries or rhubarb give the prettiest results. The tea gives the jelly a more subtle, less sweet result than normal fruit jellies. Also, it can be made up to 2 days in advance so is perfect for entertaining. If you are worried about turning it out, set the jellies in individual glasses. Don't forget to allow time for cooling and at least 2 hours' chilling.

2 sachets of fruit tea, such as
   raspberry, strawberry, loganberry
   or blackcurrant
2 tbsp caster sugar
11g/⅓oz sachet of gelatine
2 nectarines
225g/8oz raspberries, blackberries
   or loganberries
single cream, to serve

1 In a heatproof bowl, pour 600ml/1 pint boiling water over the tea sachets and put the liquid in a pan. Add the sugar and bring to the boil briefly, then remove from the heat and add the gelatine, whisking until it has completely dissolved. Set aside and leave to cool.

2 Rinse out an 850ml/1½ pint mould or bowl. Halve and stone the nectarines, then slice them thinly. Layer the nectarines and berries alternatively in the mould, then pour over the jelly and leave to set in the fridge. This will take about 2 hours.

3 To turn the jelly out, dip a cloth in very hot water and wrap it around the mould to melt the jelly slightly. Invert the mould on to a plate, then shake sharply to release the jelly. If it doesn't work, repeat the cloth trick.

4 Serve with single cream.

blueberry jelly

Preparation 10 minutes Setting 3-4 hours

Use a high-quality, real fruit blackcurrant cordial, and dilute it less than you would if drinking. If you like, you can chop the jelly up after it has set and serve it in individual glasses.

600ml/1 pint diluted blackcurrant
   cordial (see above)
1 tbsp powdered gelatine or
   3 gelatine leaves
100g/4oz blueberries

for decoration (optional)
100g/4oz blueberries
a little lightly whisked egg white
caster sugar, for dusting

1 Put a quarter of the blackcurrant liquid in a pan, sprinkle over the gelatine or crumble in the leaves, and soak for a few minutes until spongy. Heat the mixture gently, without allowing it to boil, and stir until the gelatine has all dissolved. Stir in the remaining blackcurrant liquid.

2 Pour a third of the liquid into a wetted 700ml/1¼ pint mould or 6 glasses. Add a third of the blueberries and put in the fridge until set (leave the remaining jelly at room temperature).

3 Add another third of jelly and blueberries and put in the fridge to set; then add the final third of jelly and blueberries and chill until firm.

4 If making the decoration, brush the blueberries lightly with egg white, then toss in sugar to coat. Spread over a tray lined with non-stick baking paper and leave for an hour to dry. Decorate the jelly with the frosted blueberries.

banana sesame fritters

Preparation 10 minutes Cooking 3–4 minutes

100g/3½oz self-raising flour
2 tbsp toasted sesame seeds
1 tbsp caster sugar, plus more
  for sprinkling
4 bananas, peeled
vegetable oil, for deep-frying
maple syrup, to serve

1 Mix the flour, sesame seeds and sugar in a bowl. Make a well in the centre and beat in 150ml/¼ pint of cold water to make a smooth batter.

2 Cut each banana at an angle into 4 slices. Fill a large pan or wok one-third full with oil and heat until hot. Dip the bananas in the batter, then carefully lower them into the hot oil with a slotted spoon. Fry for 3–4 minutes until crisp; drain on kitchen paper.

3 Serve the fritters hot, sprinkled with caster sugar and drizzled with some maple syrup.

candied orange puffs

Preparation 15 minutes Cooking 12–15 minutes

This is basically an Italian version of the classic French millefeuille. At one time, cut mixed peel was all you could get; now that you can get the real thing, however, the pre-cut variety seems dry and tasteless. Look for packs of citrus peel strips that are glossy and vibrant, or you may be able to buy peel loose in Italian food shops. Don't forget to allow time for the pastry to cool.

half 375g/13oz pack of ready-rolled
  puff pastry
lightly beaten egg, to glaze
250g/9oz tub of ricotta
¼ tsp ground cinnamon
60g/2oz icing sugar, plus more for
  dusting
rind and juice of 1 small orange
60g/2oz candied peel, chopped

1 Preheat the oven to 220°C/425°F/Gas 7. Roll the pastry out to a 23x38cm/ 9x15 inch oblong; cut in half lengthwise.

2 Put the pastry strips, a little apart, on a dampened baking sheet. Mark criss-cross lines over one strip with a sharp knife, taking care not to cut right through. Brush lightly with egg.

3 Bake for 12–15 minutes until golden. Carefully remove from the tray and allow to cool on a wire rack.

4 Beat together the ricotta, cinnamon and icing sugar. Stir in the orange rind and juice and all but 1 tablespoon of the peel.

5 Cut each pastry strip into four, then put one plain piece on each plate and spoon over a quarter of the filling. Set a criss-crossed piece of pastry at an angle on top. Scatter over a little peel and sift over a little icing sugar.

berry clafoutis

Preparation 15 minutes Cooking 30–40 minutes

Serve this pudding hot, straight from the oven. It's delicious with chilled thick Greek-style yoghurt.

140g/5oz plain flour
3 eggs
300ml/½ pint milk
85g/3oz caster sugar,
　plus extra for dusting
1 tsp vanilla essence
25g/1oz butter
250g/9oz mixed redcurrants
　and raspberries

1 Preheat the oven to 200°C/400°F/Gas 6.

2 Sift the flour into a bowl and make a well in it. Add the eggs and half the milk to the well, then stir with a wooden spoon from the centre, gradually drawing in the flour from the sides to make a thick batter. Stir in the sugar, remaining milk and vanilla.

3 Put the butter in a 2 litre/3½ pint ovenproof dish and place in the oven for about 2–3 minutes until the butter is melted. Pour in the batter, then sprinkle over the fruit. Bake for 30–40 minutes.

4 Dust with sugar to serve.

hot sticky apples

Preparation 10 minutes Cooking 10–12 minutes

50g/2oz unsalted butter
4 large eating apples, peeled,
　quartered and thickly sliced
3 heaped tbsp light muscovado
　sugar
grated zest of ½ orange and juice
　of 2 oranges
3 tbsp calvados or brandy
vanilla ice cream, to serve

1 Heat the butter in a frying pan and toss in the apples. Fry for about 5 minutes, until softened and tinged with brown.

2 Sprinkle in the sugar. Add the orange zest and juice, and bubble up, stirring gently. Cook for 2 minutes until the sauce starts to thicken and coats the apples with a shiny glaze.

3 Measure the calvados or brandy into a small cup (or use a miniature), quickly pour the alcohol into the pan and carefully ignite. Swirl the pan until the flames die down.

4 Serve warm over scoops of vanilla ice cream.

blackberry cinnamon meringues

Preparation 10 minutes Cooking 15–20 minutes

This beautifully simple dessert makes the most of blackberries while they're there for the picking. Late-season raspberries work really well with this too.

30g/1oz brown breadcrumbs
½ tsp ground cinnamon
225g/8oz blackberries
whites of 2 eggs
85g/3oz light muscovado sugar

❶ Preheat the oven to 190°C/375°F/Gas 5. Heat a small frying pan over a medium heat. Sprinkle the breadcrumbs and cinnamon into the pan and dry-fry, stirring occasionally, until toasted and crisp. Remove from the heat, toss with the blackberries and set aside.

❷ Whisk the egg whites to stiff peaks. Continue whisking, adding about half of the sugar, until the mixture is stiff and glossy. Fold in the remaining sugar.

❸ Lightly fold the blackberries and breadcrumbs into the meringue and spoon the mixture into four 8cm/3 inch ramekins.

❹ Bake for 15–20 minutes until golden.

redcurrant and gooseberry compote

Serves 6

Preparation 15 minutes Cooking 5 minutes

Just fruit cooked in heavy syrup, compotes are wonderfully versatile; you can serve the fruits spooned over muesli and yoghurt for breakfast, and over ice cream, meringue or sponge cake for dessert. Remember that you will need to make this a day ahead to allow time for cooling and 24 hours' chilling.

500g/1lb 2oz redcurrants
500g/1lb 2oz dessert gooseberries
175g/6oz caster sugar
juice of ½ lemon
1 tbsp cornflour

❶ Rinse the fruit, then strip the redcurrants from their stems and top and tail the gooseberries.

❷ Put the sugar, lemon juice and 400ml/14fl oz water in a pan and stir over a low heat to dissolve the sugar, then bring to a simmer. Add the gooseberries and return the syrup to a simmer. Add the redcurrants and, when the syrup is simmering again, cook the fruit very gently for no more than 1–2 minutes. Remove from the heat.

❸ Using a slotted spoon, transfer the fruit from the syrup to a bowl. Blend the cornflour with 2 tablespoons of cold water and stir into the syrup in the pan.

❹ Return the pan to the heat and bring back to the boil, stirring all the time. When clear and lightly thickened, pour the syrup over the fruit.

❺ Leave until cold, then chill for 24 hours.

baked jamaica

Preparation 15 minutes Cooking 5 minutes

Take the ice cream straight from the freezer just before you want to use it, so that it is nice and cold. Also, make sure that there are no gaps in the meringue covering, or the oven's heat will get to the ice cream and make it melt.

227g/8oz can of pineapple chunks
  in natural juice
1 Jamaica ginger cake
whites of 3 eggs
175g/6oz light muscovado sugar
500ml/18fl oz tub of vanilla ice cream

1. Preheat the oven to 220°C/425°F/Gas 7. Drain the pineapple chunks, reserving 3 tablespoons of juice. Slice the ginger cake in half horizontally and lay the slices side by side in a shallow rectangular ovenproof dish. Drizzle over the reserved pineapple juice and scatter the pineapple evenly over the cake.

2. Using an electric hand blender, whisk the egg whites until stiff. Whisk in the sugar, a tablespoon at a time, whisking well between each addition, until the meringue is thick and glossy.

3. Transfer the ice cream to a chopping board, cut it in half horizontally and lay the pieces side by side on top of the pineapple, pressing them down to level. Completely cover with the whole thing with meringue, swirling the top with a fork.

4. Bake for 5 minutes until golden. Serve at once.

mandarin and ginger sorbet

Preparation 15 minutes Cooking 5 minutes

You'll need to freeze this sorbet for at least 7–8 hours.

225g/8oz caster sugar
finely grated zest of 1 mandarin,
  plus juice of 10 mandarins
juice of 2 lemons
25g/¾oz preserved stem ginger,
  drained and finely chopped
fresh mint leaves, to decorate

1. Place the sugar in a pan and add 200ml/7fl oz water. Slowly bring to the boil, stirring until the sugar has dissolved. Boil for 5 minutes until lightly syrupy. Set aside to cool.

2. Stir in the mandarin zest and juice, the lemon juice and the stem ginger, and mix well.

3. Pour into a freezer-proof container, cover and freeze for 2-3 hours, until ice crystals are just beginning to form.

4. Remove from the freezer and beat with a wooden spoon until smooth. Return to the freezer and freeze for a further 5 hours until firm.

5. Remove from the freezer about 30 minutes before serving. Decorate with the mint leaves.

One of the easiest ways to provide a **sumptuous dessert** in a flash is with **ice cream** – be it homemade and nestling in the freezer or good ready-made grabbed on the way home. Serve it on a **bought meringue base** or drizzled with one of our **quick ice cream sauces below**, and no one will even think of it as 'just ice cream'. If you can't even be bothered to try one of the sauces, a **dash of liqueur and/or cassis** will dress most ice creams and sorbets very effectively. Don't forget how really nice **crêpes à la dentelles, boudoir or amaretti biscuits** will raise a bowl of ice cream to restaurant level – or try just a sprinkling of a few pieces of chocolate-coated peel or ginger or some shaved dark chocolate.

No-cook berry sauces can be made in a trice by simply puréeing some **raspberries, strawberries, blueberries, stoned cherries** or a mixture of seasonal soft fruit. Pass through a sieve to remove pips, add a little lemon juice and zest to taste and sweeten with icing sugar or honey. Some **fruit brandy or liqueur** will give an even more luxurious result. These are good with most ice creams and sorbets.

Raisin and honey sauce involves merely heating about 3 table-spoons of a good-quality **runny honey** in a small pan together with a dash of **brandy or grappa**. Then stir in a good handful of **seedless raisins** and mix well until these are thoroughly coated. This rich sauce is particularly wonderful with pistachio ice cream and mango sorbet.

Quick chocolate sauce is made by melting about 30g/1oz **unsalted butter** in a small pan together with 2 tablespoons of water. Break in 85g/3oz of the **best-quality dark chocolate** and stir until smooth. Then stir in 2 tablespoons of **thick cream**. You can give the chocolate sauce even more flavour with some finely **chopped stem ginger or a little green ginger wine**, or even a dash of brandy or liqueur like amaretto or crème de menthe. This sauce is best served on vanilla, ginger or mint ice cream, but goes with most.

Other quick dishes that will help bought ice cream go further and look more spectacular:
Irish Coffee Sundaes (page 104)
Oranges in Ginger Caramel (page 114)
Banana Sesame Fritters (page 118)
Berry Clafoutis (page 121)
Hot Sticky Apples (page 121)
Redcurrant and Gooseberry Compote (page 122)
Blackberry Cinnamon Meringues (page 122)

6

Depending on shop-bought biscuits and cakes can cost
a fortune over time, and they are also guaranteed to be
chock-full of unhealthy fats and additives. However busy
you are, you can always find the odd ten minutes to rustle
up some of the toothsome titbits in this chapter, and then
you'll have lots of reduced-guilt treats to hand.

trouble-free teatime treats

choc chunk peanut butter cookies

Makes 18

Preparation 15 minutes Cooking 15 minutes

Roasting the peanuts before adding them to the cookie mixture brings out their flavour. You could use ready-roasted unsalted peanuts. Use a plain chocolate containing at least 50 per cent cocoa solids for its flavour and melting qualities (it doesn't burn while cooking). Higher cocoa solids give a more pronounced chocolate taste.

85g/3oz shelled peanuts
175g/6oz plain chocolate
85g/3oz crunchy peanut butter
175g/6oz butter, softened
175g/6oz light muscovado sugar
300g/10oz self-raising flour
2 tbsp milk

1 Preheat the oven to 180°C/350°F/Gas 4. Put the peanuts in a roasting tin and roast for 10 minutes until golden. Meanwhile, line 2 or 3 baking sheets with non-stick baking parchment. (If you don't have several sheets, bake the cookies in batches using the same parchment.)

2 Rub the peanuts between your hands to remove the papery skins. Discard the skins and set the peanuts to one side.

3 Roughly chop the chocolate and two-thirds of the peanuts.

4 In a bowl, beat together the peanut butter, butter and sugar, until light and fluffy. Stir in the flour and milk with a wooden spoon, and mix well.

5 Stir in the chopped chocolate and nuts with the spoon. Bring the mixture together with your hands and divide the mixture into 18 equal portions.

6 Roughly shape each portion of dough into a ball. Put on the lined baking sheets, well spaced out to allow for spread. Lightly flatten each cookie with the prongs of a fork, then sprinkle a few of the remaining peanuts on top.

7 Bake for 12–15 minutes, until the cookies are pale golden around the edges, but still feel soft in the centre.

8 Leave to cool for about 5 minutes, then transfer to a rack and let cool a little longer before eating. They'll keep up to 1 week in an airtight tin.

lemon and sultana cookies

Makes 30

Preparation 15 minutes Cooking 12–15 minutes

140g/5oz butter, cut into small
    pieces, plus more for greasing
350g/12oz plain flour
½ tsp baking powder
½ tsp bicarbonate of soda
175g/6oz caster sugar
85g/3oz sultanas
100g/4oz lemon curd
2 eggs, beaten

for the icing
100g/4oz sifted icing sugar
2 tbsp fresh lemon juice

1 Preheat the oven to 200°C/400°F/Gas 6. Grease 3 baking sheets (if you only have one, you can bake the cookies in batches).

2 Sift the flour, baking powder and bicarbonate of soda into a bowl. Add the butter and rub in with your fingertips until the mixture resembles fine bread-crumbs. Stir in the sugar and sultanas. Add the lemon curd and eggs and mix to a soft dough. Shape the dough into 30 small balls, about 2.5 cm/1 inch wide, and put on the baking sheets, allowing plenty of space between them for spread. Gently press the top of each biscuit to flatten it slightly.

3 Bake for 12–15 minutes, until risen and light golden.

4 Leave to cool for 1 minute on the baking sheets, then transfer to a wire rack to cool completely.

5 Make the icing: blend the icing sugar and lemon juice until smooth, then drizzle over each cookie. Leave to set. The cookies are best eaten within 2 days, or freeze any that are left over.

chunky choc orange cookies

Makes 18

Preparation 15 minutes Cooking 15–20 minutes

Eat these while they're still warm – that way the chocolate is still gorgeously gooey in the middle.

250g/9oz butter, softened
55g/1¾oz caster sugar
100g/3½oz light muscovado sugar
300g/10½oz self-raising flour
2 tbsp milk
175g/6oz orange-flavoured plain
   chocolate, very roughly chopped
55g/1¾oz pecan nuts, very roughly
   chopped

① Preheat the oven to 180°C/350°F/Gas 4. Line 2 or 3 baking sheets with non-stick baking parchment. (You will probably get 7 or 8 cookies to a sheet – if you don't have enough baking sheets, bake in batches using the same baking parchment.)

② In a bowl, beat together the butter and sugars until light and fluffy (this is easy if you use an electric whisk). Stir in the flour and milk, mix well, then stir in the chocolate and nuts.

③ Divide the mixture into equal portions. To make 18 large biscuits, weigh a 50g/1⅔ oz piece of dough for each. Roughly shape the portions of dough into balls. Put on the baking sheets, well spaced out to allow for spreading. Lightly flatten each biscuit with your fingertips, keeping the mixture quite rough-looking.

④ Bake for 15–20 minutes, until the cookies are pale-golden around the edges, but still feel soft in the centre.

⑤ Allow to cool on the baking sheets for 5 minutes, then transfer to a wire rack and allow to cool a little more before eating.

classic flapjacks

Makes 12

Opinion is strongly divided as to the perfect flapjack. Some prefer theirs thick and chewy; others thin and crisp. By using different-sized tins and varying the cooking time, this recipe can be adapted to suit all tastes. You can buy jumbo oats or the smaller porridge oats, such as Quaker oats. Both can be used in this recipe, but give slightly different results. The larger oats absorb less liquid, so the flapjacks tend to have a pronounced butteriness and a more crunchy texture. The smaller oats give a more compact, chewy bar.

175g/6oz butter, cut into pieces
150g/5oz golden syrup
55g/2oz light muscovado sugar
250g/9oz oats

1 Preheat the oven to 180°C/350°F/Gas 4. Line the base of a shallow 23cm/9 inch square tin with a sheet of baking parchment if the tin is not non-stick (or use a 20cm/8 inch square tin for a thicker, chewier flapjack).
2 Put the butter, syrup and sugar in a medium pan. Stir over a low heat until the butter has melted and the sugar has dissolved. Remove from the heat and stir in the oats.
3 Press the mixture into the tin. Bake for 20–25 minutes, until golden brown on top (follow the longer cooking time for a crisper flapjack).
4 Allow to cool in the tin for 5 minutes, then mark into bars or squares with the back of a knife while still warm. Leave to cool completely in the tin before cutting and removing – this prevents the flapjack from breaking up.

oaty cherry cookies

Makes 18

Allow time for these cookies to cool completely. They can then be stored for up to 2 days in an airtight container.

250g/9oz butter, softened
50g/1¾oz caster sugar
100g/3½oz light muscovado sugar
150g /5½oz self-raising flour
225g/8oz porridge oats
200g/7oz glacé cherries
50g/1¾oz raisins

1 Preheat the oven to 180°C/350°F/Gas 4. Line 2 or 3 baking sheets with non-stick baking parchment (or use one sheet and bake in batches).
2 In a bowl, beat the butter and sugars together until light and fluffy. Stir in the flour and oats and mix well. Roughly chop three-quarters of the cherries, then stir these and the whole cherries and raisins into the oat mixture.
3 Roughly shape the mixture into balls and arrange on the baking sheet(s), well spaced out to allow for spreading. Lightly flatten each biscuit with your fingertips. Bake for 15–20 minutes, until pale-golden but still slightly soft in the centre.
4 Allow the cookies to cool for 5 minutes on the baking sheet(s), then transfer to a wire rack and allow to cool completely before serving.

muffins in minutes

The good old-fashioned Victorian **muffin**, toasted and served with butter for tea, has lately been reinvented by our American cousins, emerging **packed full of fruit** and other goodies to make **great breakfast treats or snacks** for any time of the day.

The secrets of success with muffins: first you must get the right kind of deep-recess muffin tins; ordinary little bun tins are just not big enough to give the right sort of results. Secondly, you must grease the recesses well, or get a non-stick tin. As the mixture used is generally a batter rather than a dough, this type of muffin is at its best on the day it is made; they are not really designed to be stored – so, go on, have another!

Blueberry buttermilk muffins: in a large bowl, combine 400g/14oz plain flour, 175g/6oz caster sugar, 1 tbsp baking powder, the finely grated zest of 1 lemon and ½ tsp salt. In a separate bowl, mix together 284ml/10fl oz buttermilk, 2 beaten eggs and 85g/3oz melted butter. Make a well in the centre of the dry ingredients and pour in the buttermilk mixture. Stir until just combined and quite stiff, but don't overmix. Lightly fold in 250g/9oz fresh or frozen blueberries, or mixed summer fruits, then spoon the mixture into 12 buttered holes in a muffin tin to fill generously.

Bake in an oven preheated to 200°C/400°F/Gas 6 for about 25 minutes, until well risen and pale-golden on top. Leave to cool in the tin for about 5 minutes, then turn out on to a wire rack.

To make **triple chocolate chunk muffins**: combine 250g/9oz plain flour, 30g/1oz cocoa powder, 2 tsp baking powder, ½ tsp bicarbonate of soda and 85g/3oz each dark and white chocolate, broken into chunks in a large bowl. In another bowl, mix together 2 beaten eggs, 284ml/10fl oz carton of soured cream, 85g/3oz light muscovado sugar and 85g/3oz melted butter. Add the soured cream mixture to the flour mixture and stir until just combined and the mixture is fairly stiff, but don't overmix. Spoon the mixture into 11 buttered holes on a muffin tin to fill generously. Bake and cool as above.

Blackberry muffins (opposite): in a large bowl, combine 400g/14oz plain flour, 175g/6oz caster sugar, 1 tbsp baking powder, the finely grated zest of 1 orange and ½ tsp salt. In a separate bowl, mix together 284ml/10 fl oz carton of buttermilk, 2 beaten eggs and 85g/3oz melted butter. Make a well in the centre of the dry ingredients and pour in the buttermilk mixture. Stir until the ingredients are just combined and the mixture is quite stiff, but don't overmix. Lightly fold in 250g/9oz fresh or frozen blackberries, or mixed summer fruits, then spoon the mixture into 12 buttered holes in a muffin tin to fill generously.

Bake the muffins in an oven preheated to 200°C/400°F/Gas 6 for 15–18 minutes, until they are well risen and pale-golden on top. Leave them to cool in the tin for a few minutes, then turn them out carefully on to a wire rack to allow them to cool further.

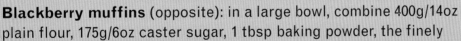
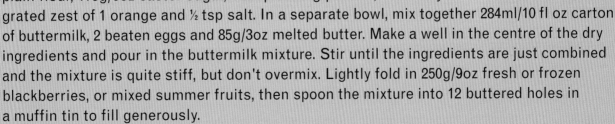

portuguese custard tarts

Preparation 10 minutes Cooking 35 minutes

If you've never tasted these tarts before, you're in for a real treat. Irresistibly crisp, sugary pastry shells are filled with thick, creamy custard, heavily sugared and grilled to make a caramel glaze.

450g/1lb puff pastry
425ml/15fl oz carton of custard
2 tsp vanilla extract
2 medium eggs, beaten
25g/¾oz icing sugar

1 Preheat the oven to 190°C/375°F/Gas 5. Roll the pastry out to 30x40cm/ 12x16 inches. Using a plain pastry cutter, cut out twelve 10cm/4 inch circles and use to line a muffin tin.

2 In a jug, beat together the custard, vanilla extract and eggs, and then pour the mixture into the pastry cases.

3 Bake for 35–40 minutes, then allow to cool completely in the muffin tin.

4 Preheat the grill to high. Dust the tarts with the icing sugar and grill for 5 minutes, until the sugar is caramelized and lightly charred.

peach and almond crescents

Makes 6

Preparation 15 minutes Cooking about 15 minutes

Ready-to-bake croissant dough can be found in most supermarket chill cabinets.

butter, for greasing
1 peach
juice from 1 lemon
240g/9oz packet of ready-to-bake
  croissant dough
85g/3oz marzipan
2 tbsp flaked almonds
icing sugar, for dusting
extra-thick double cream or clotted
  cream, to serve

1 Preheat the oven to 200°C/400°F/Gas 6 and lightly grease a baking sheet. Peel the peach, slice it thinly and put into a small bowl. Squeeze the juice from the lemon and drizzle half of it over the peach slices.

2 Unroll the dough and cut along the perforations to make 6 triangles, following the instructions on the packet.

3 Divide the marzipan into 6 pieces. Put one triangle square-on to you, with its point at the top; flatten it slightly. Put a marzipan piece along the triangle's base. Divide the peach slices between the triangles. Roll up from the base to the point, quite tightly, to form a crescent shape. Put on the greased baking sheet and brush with the remaining lemon juice. Sprinkle each crescent with flaked almonds.

4 Bake for about 15 minutes, until the dough is risen and golden-brown.

5 Dust with icing sugar and serve with spoonfuls of extra-thick double cream or clotted cream.

no-bake choc crunchies

Makes 8–10 (easily doubled)

Preparation 15 minutes, plus 30 minutes chilling

These are perfect for lunch boxes.

100g/3½oz butter, plus more
   for the tin
200g/7oz digestive biscuits
3 tbsp golden syrup
2 tbsp cocoa powder
60g/2oz raisins
100g/3½oz plain chocolate

1. Butter an 18cm/7 inch sandwich tin.
2. Seal the biscuits in a strong polythene bag and bash into uneven crumbs with a rolling pin.
3. Melt the butter and syrup in a pan (or microwave on High for about 1½ minutes). Stir in the cocoa and raisins, then thoroughly stir in the biscuit crumbs. Spoon into the tin and press down firmly.
4. Melt the chocolate in a heatproof bowl set over a pan of simmering water (or microwave on Medium for 2½ minutes). Spread over the biscuit base.
5. Chill for about half an hour. Cut into wedges to serve. This will keep for up to 1 week wrapped in foil.

mocha hazelnut meringue gâteau

Serves 6–8

Preparation 15 minutes Cooking 1 hour

whites of 4 eggs
200g/7oz golden caster sugar
100g/3½oz toasted hazelnuts,
   finely chopped
175g/6oz dark chocolate, broken
   into pieces
2 tbsp cold strong black coffee
450ml/¾ pint double cream
icing sugar, for dusting

1. Preheat the oven to 150°C/300°F/Gas 2. Whisk the egg whites into stiff peaks, then add the sugar in batches, whisking after each addition, until you have a stiff, glossy meringue. Lightly fold in the hazelnuts.
2. Line 3 baking sheets with baking parchment and draw a 20cm/8 inch diameter circle on each. Turn over and spread the meringue up to the lines.
3. Bake for 1 hour, then allow to cool in the oven.
4. Melt the chocolate with the coffee in a bowl set over a pan of hot water. Allow to cool at room temperature.
5. Whisk the cream until thickened; then whisk in the chocolate. Sandwich the cooled meringues together with the mocha cream.
6. Dust with icing sugar to serve.

acknowledgments

Recipes by

Lorna Brash
Chicory, bean and chilli crostini p43, Soft polenta with pak choi and soy dressing p96, Chocolate baked ricotta p101, Portuguese custard tarts p136

Fern Britton
Spinach soup with crunchy garlic bread p25

Sara Buenfeld
Pan-seared pork stroganoff with porcini pasta twists p77, Rustic noodles with cabbage, anchovies and melted cheese p95

Mary Cadogan
Prawn and mango cocktail p14, Melon with mint, ginger and orange p14, Cod with lemon and parsley sauce p52, Lemon barbecued lamb with haricot mash p78, Tomato and olive chicken p80, Salmon with tarragon cream sauce p88, Plaice goujouns in a tea batter p92, Velvet chocolate torte p102, Ten-minute tiramisu p104, Fruit tea jelly p117, Candied orange puffs p118, Lemon and sultana cookies p130

Richard Cawley
Creamy mushrooms on toasted brioche p21, Irish coffee sundaes p104

Sally Clarke
Goats' cheese and thyme soufflés p96

Shona Crawford Poole
Blueberry jelly p117

Gilly Cubitt
Haloumi and tomato wraps p45

Matthew Drennan
Spiced Seville duck p82

Lewis Esson
Kung pao prawns p17

Joanna Farrow
Gnocchi with broad beans and mushrooms p21

Silvana Franco
Beef sukiyaki p70

Susanna Gelmetti
Orange semi-freddo with orange sauce p114

Mark Gregory
Tofu miso soup p28, from his restaurant Axis at One Aldwych Hotel

Good Food Team
Roast asparagus and prosciutto bundles p12, Fried prawns with chilli and lime leaf, Pea and watercress soup p23, Tomato salsa soup p23, Courgette, basil and Brie soup p27, Las Vegas gumbo p27, Black bean broth with soba noodles p28, Mediterranean rice salad p33, Olive pesto pasta p36, Skewered lamb with naan bread p38, Italian burgers p38, Tuna, bean and sweetcorn salad p41, Chicken liver, bacon and mushroom toasts p41, Croque monsieur p43, Lemon, artichoke and feta khobez p44, Chicken tortilla pouches p45, Scrambled smokies p46, Quick fish risotto p46, Minted pea omelette p48, Great American brunch p49, Cheese and mustard crusted cod p52, Crisp mustard cod p53, Crunchy-topped fish pie p55, Plaice and crispy bacon grill p55, Chicken and broccoli noodles p57, Lemon prawn pan-fry p57, Barbecued coriander chicken with guacamole salsa p58, Chicken tarragon pasta p58, Lamb chop and spicy chip bake p61, Teriyaki chicken and vegetable bake p61, Spicy roast chicken p62, Chinese turkey kebabs with 4-minute noodles p63, Creamy ham and bean stew p65, Creamy spaghetti with bacon and courgette p65, Spicy sausage pasta p66, Lamb and spring onion stir-fry p68, Lamb and date casserole p68, Lemon and oregano pork p76, Rolled pork slices p76, Minted lamb with couscous p78, Duck casserole with herbed new potatoes p82, Italian cod and garlic tomatoes p85, Fish salad with lemon basil dressing p85, Griddled salmon with lime and chilli butter p88, Spring herb salmon with warm tomato dressing p91, Baked salmon with preserved lemon chermoula p91, Grilled trout with cashew and garlic butter p92, Speedy rice pudding brûlées p107, Rhubarb and strawberry cream fool p108, Strawberry crush p108, Summer berry brûlée p110, Raspberry cream with crunchy caramelized oats p110, Blackberry sherry creams p113, Banana sesame fritters p118, Berry clafoutis p121, Hot sticky apples p121, Baked Jamaica p124, Chunky choc orange cookies p131, Oaty cherry cookies p132, Peach and almond crescents p136, No-bake choc crunchies p139, Mocha hazelnut meringue gâteau p139

Alastair Hendy
Black bean roasted sea bass with ginger p87

Mai nGoc Henry
Mandarin and ginger sorbet p124

Catherine Hill
Broad bean, feta and radicchio salad p35, Roasted asparagus and tomato Thai salad p37, Souffléed olive and avocado omelette p48, Indian chickpea salad p97

Clare Lewis
Mixed leaves with feta and griddled peaches p18, Pak choi and carrot rösti p95

Sara Lewis
Chocolate baskets with berries p101

Kate Moseley
Sausage, bacon and bean bake p66

Orlando Murrin
Roast asparagus with garlic and capers p12, Fig and goats' cheese salad p18, Lettuce soup p24, Stuffed marrow p73, Croissant and chocolate pudding p102

Vicky Musselman
Choc chunk peanut butter cookies p130, Blackberry muffins p135

Angela Nilsen
Prêt's tuna mayo pasta salad p35, New Mexican chilli p71, Chicken with prosciutto and fried sage leaves p81, Classic flapjacks p132, Blueberry buttermilk muffins p135, Triple chocolate chunk muffins p135

Angela Nilsen and Jenny White
Pan-fried red mullet fillets with chilli ginger dressing p87

Bridget Sargeson
Marinated peppers and chillies in oil p32, Marinated peppers with prosciutto and pine nuts p32, Cauliflower cheese lasagne p73

Katie Stewart
Redcurrant and gooseberry compote p122

Lesley Waters
Cardamom spiced puddings p107, Oranges in ginger caramel p114

Jenny White
Apricot and ginger snap glory p113, Blackberry cinnamon meringues p122

Photographers

Chris Alack
Lemon, artichoke and feta khobez p44

Marie-Louise Avery
Sausage, bacon and bean bake p66, Spring herb salmon with warm tomato dressing p91

Clive Bozzard-Hill
Chocolate baskets with berries p100

Linda Burgess
Berries p127

Jean Cazals
Green beans with crispy parma ham p6, Fried prawns with chilli and a lime leaf p17, Creamy mushrooms on toasted brioche p21, Blender p22, Pea and watercress soup p 23, Courgette, basil and Brie soup p26, Las Vegas gumbo p27, New Mexican chilli p71, Rolled pork slices p74, Pan-seared pork stroganoff with porcini pasta twists p77, Italian cod and garlic tomatoes p84, Rustic noodles with cabbage, anchovies, and melted cheese p94, Candied orange puffs p118, Berry clafoutis p120, Redcurrant and gooseberry compote p123, Ice cream p126, Lemon and sultana cookies p129

Tim De Winter
Velvet chocolate torte p103

Gus Filgate
Kung pao prawns p16, Salmon with a glazed lemon garnish p90, Baked salmon with preserved lemon chermoula p91

Anna Hodgson
Blackberry muffins p134

Tim Imrie
Choc chunk peanut butter cookies p128

Dave King
Chocolate baked ricotta p98

David Munns
Deseeding tomatoes p8, Asparagus tips p10, Lettuce soup p24, Cardamom spiced puddings p106, Mocha hazelnut meringue gateau p139

James Murphy
Asparagus p11, Roasted asparagus and prosciutto bundles p13

Sean Myers
Pak choi and carrot rösti p95

Nick Pope
Black bean roasted sea bass with ginger p86

William Reavell
Black bean broth with soba noodles p5 and 29, Gnocchi with broad beans and mushrooms p20, Broad bean radicchio and feta salad p35, Roasted asparagus and tomato Thai salad p37, Haloumi and tomato wraps p45, Indian chickpea salad p97

Howard Shooter
Mixed leaves with feta and griddled peaches p18

Sam Stowell
Apricot and ginger snap glory p113

Roger Stowell
Melon with mint, ginger and orange pages 1 and 15, Whisking melted chocolate pages 3 and 99, Chopping onions p8, Snipping chives p8, Prawn and mango cocktail p14, Tomato salsa soup p23, Mediterranean rice salad p33, Olive pesto pasta p36, Italian burgers p38, Skewered lamb with naan bread p39, Chicken liver bacon and mushroom toasts p40, Tuna, bean and sweetcorn salad p41, Croque monsieur p42, Chicken tortilla pouches p45, Quick microwave fish risotto p46, Scrambled smokies p47, Minted pea omelette p48, Great American brunch p49, Cheese and mustard crusted cod p52, Crisp mustard cod p53, Crunchy-topped fish pie p54, Plaice and crispy bacon grill p55, Chicken and broccoli noodles p56, Chicken and broccoli noodles (and spoon) p57, Lemon prawn pan-fry p57, Barbecued coriander chicken with guacamole salsa p59, Teriyaki chicken and vegetable bake p60, Lamb chop and spicy chip bake p61, Spicy roast chicken p62, Chinese turkey kebabs with 4-minute noodles p63, Creamy spaghetti with bacon and courgettes p64, Creamy ham and bean stew p65, Spicy sausage pasta p67, Lamb and spring onion stir-fry p69, Lemon and oregano pork p75, Minted lamb with couscous p79, Salmon with tarragon cream sauce p89, Croissant and chocolate pudding p102, Speedy rice pudding brûlée p107, Rhubarb and strawberry cream fool p108, Strawberry crush p109, Raspberry cream with crunchy caramelized oats p110, Summer berry brûlée p111, Blackberry sherry creams p112, Banana sesame fritters p119, Baked Jamaica p125, Peach and almond crescents p136, No-bake chocolate crunchies p138

Ian Wallace
Fig and goats' cheese salad p19

Philip Webb
Marinated peppers with prosciutto and pine nuts p30, Marinated peppers and chillies in oil p31, Prêt's tuna mayo pasta salad p34, Cod with lemon and parsley sauce p50, Cod with lemon and parsley sauce (detail) p51, Duck casserole with herbed new potatoes p83, Plaice goujons in tea batter p93, Oranges in ginger caramel p115, Fruit tea jelly p116, Blackberry cinnamon meringues p122, Classic flapjacks p133, Blueberry buttermilk muffins p135, Triple chocolate chip muffins p135

Simon Wheeler
Ten-minute tiramisu pages 2 and 105, Cauliflower cheese lasagne p72, Tomato and olive chicken p80, Chicken with prosciutto and fried sage leaves p81, Chunky choc orange cookies p131

John Whitaker
Portugese custard tarts p137

Whilst every effort has been made to trace and acknowledge all copyright holders, we would like to apologize should there be any errors or omissions.

index

a

almonds:
    peach and almond
        crescents, 136
American brunch, 49
anchovies, rustic noodles
    with cabbage, melted
        cheese and, 95
apples, hot sticky, 121
apricot and ginger snap
    glory, 113
artichokes:
    lemon, artichoke and feta
        khobez, 45
asparagus:
    roast asparagus and
        prosciutto bundles, 12
    roast asparagus with
        garlic and capers, 12
    roasted asparagus and
        tomato Thai salad, 37
avocados:
    barbecued coriander
        chicken with guacamole
            salsa, 58
    souffléed olive and
        avocado omelette, 48

b

bacon:
    BLT burgers, 70
    chicken liver, bacon and
        mushroom toasts, 41
    creamy spaghetti with
        bacon and courgette, 65
    plaice and crispy bacon
        grill, 55
    sausage, bacon and bean
        bake, 66
baked Jamaica, 124
banana sesame fritters, 118
beans:
    chicory, bean and chilli
        crostini, 43
    chilli bean tortillas, 45
    creamy ham and bean
        stew, 65
    lemon barbecued lamb
        with haricot mash, 78
    new Mexican chilli, 71
    sausage, bacon and bean
        bake, 66
    stuffed marrow, 73
    tuna, bean and sweetcorn
        salad, 41
beef:
    beef sukiyaki, 70
    BLT burgers, 70

chilli bean tortillas, 45
beetroot:
    great American brunch, 49
berry clafoutis, 121
biscuits see cookies
black beans:
    black bean broth with soba
        noodles, 28
    black bean roasted sea
        bass with ginger, 87
blackberries:
    blackberry cinnamon
        meringues, 122
    blackberry muffins, 135
    blackberry sherry creams,
        113
BLT burgers, 70
blueberries:
    blueberry buttermilk
        muffins, 135
    blueberry jelly, 117
    chocolate baskets with
        berries, 101
bread:
    chicory, bean and chilli
        crostini, 43
    croque monsieur, 43
    crunchy garlic bread, 25
    skewered lamb with naan
        bread, 38
brioche:
    creamy mushrooms on
        toasted brioche, 21
broad beans:
    broad bean, feta and
        radicchio salad, 35
    gnocchi with mushrooms
        and, 21
broccoli:
    cauliflower cheese
        lasagne, 73
    chicken and broccoli
        noodles, 57
burgers:
    BLT burgers, 70
    Italian burgers, 38
butter beans:
    creamy ham and bean
        stew, 65
    stuffed marrow, 73
buttermilk muffins,
    blueberry, 135

c

cabbage, rustic noodles with
    anchovies, melted cheese
        and, 95
candied orange puffs, 118

cannellini beans:
    chicory, bean and chilli
        crostini, 43
    creamy ham and bean
        stew, 65
    sausage, bacon and bean
        bake, 66
caramel:
    oranges in ginger caramel,
        114
cardamom spiced puddings,
    107
carrots:
    pak choi and carrot rösti, 95
casseroles see stews
cauliflower cheese lasagne, 73
cheese:
    broad bean, feta and
        radicchio salad, 35
    cauliflower cheese
        lasagne, 73
    cheese and mustard
        crusted cod, 52
    courgette, basil and Brie
        soup, 27
    creamy spaghetti with
        bacon and courgette, 65
    croque monsieur, 43
    crunchy-topped fish pie, 55
    fig and goats' cheese
        salad, 18
    gnocchi with broad beans
        and mushrooms, 21
    goats' cheese and thyme
        soufflés, 96
    haloumi and tomato
        wraps, 45
    lemon, artichoke and feta
        khobez, 45
    mixed leaves with feta and
        griddled peaches, 18
    rustic noodles with
        cabbage, anchovies and
            melted cheese, 95
cherries:
    oaty cherry cookies, 132
chicken:
    barbecued coriander
        chicken with guacamole
            salsa, 58
    chicken and broccoli
        noodles, 57
    chicken tarragon pasta, 58
    chicken tortilla pouches, 45
    chicken with prosciutto
        and fried sage leaves, 81
    Italian burgers, 38
    Las Vegas gumbo, 27

spicy roast chicken, 62
    teriyaki chicken and
        vegetable bake, 61
    tomato and olive chicken, 80
chicken liver, bacon and
    mushroom toasts, 41
chickpea salad, Indian, 97
chicory, bean and chilli
    crostini, 43
chilli:
    chicory, bean and chilli
        crostini, 43
    chilli bean tortillas, 45
    griddled salmon with lime
        and chilli butter, 88
    Kung Pao prawns, 17
    marinated peppers and
        chillies in oil, 32
    new Mexican chilli, 71
    pan-fried red mullet fillets
        with chilli ginger
            dressing, 87
Chinese turkey kebabs with
    4-minute noodles, 63
chocolate: choc chunk
    peanut butter cookies, 130
    chocolate baked ricotta, 101
    chocolate baskets with
        berries, 101
    chunky choc orange
        cookies, 131
    croissant and chocolate
        pudding, 102
    mocha hazelnut meringue
        gâteau, 139
    no-bake choc crunchies,
        139
    quick chocolate sauce, 127
    ten-minute tiramisu, 104
    triple chocolate chunk
        muffins, 135
    velvet chocolate torte, 102
clafoutis, berry, 121
cod:
    cheese and mustard
        crusted cod, 52
    cod with lemon and
        parsley sauce, 52
    crisp mustard cod, 53
    crunchy-topped fish pie, 55
    Italian cod and garlic
        tomatoes, 85
    see also smoked cod
coffee:
    Irish coffee sundaes, 104
    mocha hazelnut meringue
        gâteau, 139
    ten-minute tiramisu, 104

cookies:
    choc chunk peanut
        butter, 130
    chunky choc orange, 131
    lemon and sultana, 130
    oaty cherry, 132
courgettes:
    courgette, basil and Brie
        soup, 27
    creamy spaghetti with
        bacon and courgette, 65
    Mediterranean rice
        salad, 33
    teriyaki chicken and
        vegetable bake, 61
couscous, minted lamb
    with, 78
croissant and chocolate
    pudding, 102
croque-monsieur, 43
crostini, chicory, bean and
    chilli, 43
curried sweet potato soup, 25
custard:
    Portuguese custard
        tarts, 136
    rhubarb and strawberry
        cream fool, 108

d

dates:
    lamb and date casserole, 68
desserts, 98–127
duck:
    duck casserole with
        herbed new potatoes, 82
    spiced Seville duck, 82

e

eggs:
    great American brunch, 49
    minted pea omelette, 48
    scrambled smokies, 46
    souffléed olive and
        avocado omelette, 48

f

fig and goats' cheese
    salad, 18
fish salad with lemon basil
    dressing, 85
flapjacks, classic, 132
fool, rhubarb and strawberry
    cream, 108
fritters, banana sesame, 118
fruit:
    no-cook berry sauces, 127
fruit tea jelly, 117

g

gammon:
creamy ham and bean
stew, 65
garlic:
grilled trout with
cashew and garlic
butter, 92
Italian cod and garlic
tomatoes, 85
roast asparagus with
capers and, 12
spinach soup with crunchy
garlic bread, 25
ginger:
apricot and ginger snap
glory, 113
baked Jamaica, 124
black bean roasted sea
bass with, 87
mandarin and ginger
sorbet, 124
melon with mint, orange
and, 14
oranges in ginger caramel,
114
pan-fried red mullet fillets
with chilli ginger
dressing, 87
gnocchi with broad
beans and mushrooms,
21
goats' cheese see cheese
gooseberries: redcurrant
and gooseberry
compote, 122
guacamole salsa, 58
gumbo, Las Vegas, 27

h

haddock see smoked
haddock
haloumi and tomato
wraps, 45
ham:
creamy ham and bean
stew, 65
croque-monsieur, 43
great American brunch,
49
haricot mash, lemon
barbecued lamb with, 78
hazelnuts:
mocha hazelnut meringue
gâteau, 139
honey:
raisin and honey sauce,
127

i

ice cream, 127
baked Jamaica, 124
Irish coffee sundaes, 104
Indian chickpea salad, 97
Irish coffee sundaes, 104
Italian burgers, 38
Italian cod and garlic
tomatoes, 85

j

jelly:
blueberry jelly, 117
fruit tea jelly, 117

k

kebabs:
Chinese turkey kebabs
with 4-minute noodles, 63
skewered lamb with naan
bread, 38
Kung Pao prawns, 17

l

lamb:
lamb and date casserole,
68
lamb and spring onion stir-
fry, 68
lamb chop and spicy chip
bake, 61
lemon barbecued lamb
with haricot mash, 78
minted lamb with
couscous, 78
skewered lamb with naan
bread, 38
lamb's lettuce and sesame
salad, 43
Las Vegas gumbo, 27
lasagne, cauliflower
cheese, 73
lemon:
baked salmon with
preserved lemon
chermoula, 91
cod with lemon and
parsley sauce, 52
fish salad with lemon basil
dressing, 85
lemon and oregano pork, 76
lemon and sultana cookies,
130
lemon, artichoke and feta
khobez, 45
lemon barbecued lamb
with haricot mash, 78
lemon prawn pan-fry, 57

lettuce:
BLT burgers, 70
lettuce soup, 24
lime and chilli butter, 88
liver see chicken liver

m

mandarin and ginger sorbet,
124
mange-tout peas: black
bean roasted sea bass
with ginger, 87
mangoes:
prawn and mango
cocktail, 14
marinated peppers and
chillies in oil, 32
marinated peppers with
prosciutto and pine
nuts, 32
marrow, stuffed, 73
marzipan:
peach and almond
crescents, 136
mascarpone:
blackberry sherry
creams, 113
rustic noodles with
cabbage, anchovies
and melted cheese, 95
ten-minute tiramisu, 104
mayonnaise:
prawn and mango
cocktail, 14
Prêt's tuna mayo pasta
salad, 35
Mediterranean rice
salad, 33
melon with mint, ginger
and orange, 14
meringues:
baked Jamaica, 124
blackberry cinnamon
meringues, 122
mocha hazelnut meringue
gâteau, 139
Mexican chilli, 71
miso:
tofu miso soup, 28
mocha hazelnut meringue
gâteau, 139
muffins:
blackberry muffins, 135
blueberry buttermilk
muffins, 135
scrambled smokies, 46
triple chocolate chunk
muffins, 135

mushrooms:
chicken liver, bacon and
mushroom toasts, 41
creamy mushrooms on
toasted brioche, 21
gnocchi with broad beans
and, 21
pan-seared pork
stroganoff with porcini
pasta twists, 77
mustard:
cheese and mustard
crusted cod, 52
crisp mustard cod, 53

n

no-cook soups, 23
noodles:
black bean broth with soba
noodles, 28
chicken and broccoli
noodles, 57
Chinese turkey kebabs
with 4-minute noodles, 63
roasted asparagus and
tomato Thai salad, 37
rustic noodles with
cabbage, anchovies and
melted cheese, 95

o

oats:
classic flapjacks, 132
oaty cherry cookies, 132
raspberry cream with
crunchy caramelized
oats, 110
olives:
olive pesto pasta, 36
souffléed olive and
avocado omelette, 48
tomato and olive
chicken, 80
omelettes:
minted pea omelette, 48
souffléed olive and
avocado omelette, 48
orange:
candied orange puffs, 118
chunky choc orange
cookies, 131
hot sticky apples, 121
mandarin and ginger
sorbet, 124
melon with mint, ginger
and orange, 14
orange semi-freddo with
orange sauce, 114

oranges in ginger caramel,
114
spiced Seville duck, 82

p

pak choi:
pak choi and carrot
rösti, 95
soft polenta with pak
choi and soy dressing, 96
parsnips:
spicy roast chicken, 62
pasta:
broad bean, feta and
radicchio salad, 35
cauliflower cheese
lasagne, 73
chicken tarragon pasta, 58
creamy spaghetti with
bacon and courgette, 65
olive pesto pasta, 36
pan-seared pork
stroganoff with porcini
pasta twists, 77
Prêt's tuna mayo pasta
salad, 35
spicy sausage pasta, 66
pastries:
candied orange puffs, 118
peach and almond
crescents, 136
Portuguese custard
tarts, 136
peaches:
mixed leaves with feta
and griddled peaches, 18
peach and almond
crescents, 136
speedy rice pudding
brûlées, 107
peanuts:
choc chunk peanut butter
cookies, 130
peas:
crunchy-topped fish pie, 55
duck casserole with
herbed new potatoes, 82
minted pea omelette, 48
pea and watercress
soup, 23
see also mange-tout peas
peppers:
chicken tortilla pouches, 45
marinated peppers and
chillies in oil, 32
marinated peppers with
prosciutto and pine
nuts, 32

teriyaki chicken and vegetable bake, 61
pesto:
  olive pesto pasta, 36
pineapple:
  baked Jamaica, 124
pinto beans:
  new Mexican chilli, 71
plaice:
  plaice and crispy bacon grill, 55
  plaice goujons in a tea batter, 92
polenta with pak choi and soy dressing, 96
pork:
  lemon and oregano pork, 76
  new Mexican chilli, 71
  pan-seared pork stroganoff with porcini pasta twists, 77
  rolled pork slices, 76
Portuguese custard tarts, 136
potatoes:
  duck casserole with herbed new potatoes, 82
  great American brunch, 49
  lamb chop and spicy chip bake, 61
  pak choi and carrot rösti, 95
prawns:
  fish salad with lemon basil dressing, 85
  fried prawns with chilli and lime leaf, 17
  Kung Pao prawns, 17
  Las Vegas gumbo, 27
  lemon prawn pan-fry, 57
  prawn and mango cocktail, 14
Prêt's tuna mayo pasta salad, 35
prosciutto:
  chicken with fried sage leaves and, 81
  fig and goats' cheese salad, 18
  marinated peppers with pine nuts and, 32
  roast asparagus and prosciutto bundles, 12
  rolled pork slices, 76

r
raisin and honey sauce, 127
raspberries:
  berry clafoutis, 121

chocolate baskets with berries, 101
fruit tea jelly, 117
raspberry cream with crunchy caramelized oats, 110
summer berry brûlée, 110
red kidney beans:
  chilli bean tortillas, 45
  new Mexican chilli, 71
  tuna, bean and sweetcorn salad, 41
red mullet, pan-fried with chilli ginger dressing, 87
redcurrants:
  berry clafoutis, 121
  redcurrant and gooseberry compote, 122
rhubarb and strawberry cream fool, 108
rice:
  beef sukiyaki, 70
  cardamom spiced puddings, 107
  Las Vegas gumbo, 27
  Mediterranean rice salad, 33
  quick microwave fish risotto, 46
  speedy rice pudding brûlées, 107
ricotta:
  candied orange puffs, 118
  chocolate baked ricotta, 101
risotto, quick microwave fish, 46
rösti, pak choi and carrot, 95

s
salads:
  barbecued coriander chicken with guacamole salsa, 58
  broad bean, feta and radicchio salad, 35
  fig and goats' cheese salad, 18
  fish salad with lemon basil dressing, 85
  Indian chickpea salad, 97
  lamb's lettuce and sesame salad, 43
  Mediterranean rice salad, 33
  mixed leaves with feta and griddled peaches, 18
  Prêt's tuna mayo pasta salad, 35
  roasted asparagus and tomato Thai salad, 37

tomato and chive salad, 52
tuna, bean and sweetcorn salad, 41
salmon, 91
  baked salmon with preserved lemon chermoula, 91
  griddled salmon with lime and chilli butter, 88
  salmon with tarragon cream sauce, 88
  spring herb salmon with warm tomato dressing, 91
  see also smoked salmon
salsa, guacamole, 58
sauces:
  no-cook berry sauces, 127
  quick chocolate sauce, 127
  raisin and honey sauce, 127
sausages:
  sausage, bacon and bean bake, 66
  spicy sausage pasta, 66
scrambled smokies, 46
sea bass, black bean roasted, 87
sesame seeds:
  banana sesame fritters, 118
  lamb's lettuce and sesame salad, 43
smoked cod:
  quick microwave fish risotto, 46
smoked haddock:
  scrambled smokies, 46
smoked salmon:
  fish salad with lemon basil dressing, 85
sorbet, mandarin and ginger, 124
soufflés, goats' cheese and thyme, 96
soups:
  black bean broth with soba noodles, 28
  courgette, basil and Brie soup, 27
  curried sweet potato soup, 25
  Las Vegas gumbo, 27
  lettuce soup, 24
  no-cook soups, 23
  pea and watercress soup, 23
  spinach soup with crunchy garlic bread, 25
  tofu miso soup, 28
  tomato salsa soup, 23
  tortilla soup, 23

spaghetti with bacon and courgette, 65
spinach:
  pan-fried red mullet fillets with chilli ginger dressing, 87
  spinach soup with crunchy garlic bread, 25
spring onions:
  lamb and spring onion stir-fry, 68
stews:
  creamy ham and bean stew, 65
  duck casserole with herbed new potatoes, 82
  lamb and date casserole, 68
stir-fries, 57
strawberries:
  rhubarb and strawberry cream fool, 108
  strawberry crush, 108
  summer berry brûlée, 110
sukiyaki sauce, 70
summer berry brûlée, 110
sundaes, Irish coffee, 104
sweet potato soup, curried, 25

t
tarts, Portuguese custard, 136
tea:
  fruit tea jelly, 117
  plaice goujons in a tea batter, 92
ten-minute tiramisu, 104
teriyaki chicken and vegetable bake, 61
tiramisu, ten-minute, 104
toasts, chicken liver, bacon and mushroom, 41
tofu miso soup, 28
tomatoes:
  BLT burgers, 70
  chilli bean tortillas, 45
  fish salad with lemon basil dressing, 85
  haloumi and tomato wraps, 45
  Italian cod and garlic tomatoes, 85
  roasted asparagus and tomato Thai salad, 37
  spicy sausage pasta, 66
  spring herb salmon with warm tomato dressing, 91
  stuffed marrow, 73
  tomato and chive salad, 52
  tomato and olive chicken, 80

tomato salsa soup, 23
tortilla soup, 23
torte, velvet chocolate, 102
tortillas:
  chicken tortilla pouches, 45
  chilli bean tortillas, 45
  tortilla soup, 23
trout grilled with cashew and garlic butter, 92
tuna:
  Prêt's tuna mayo pasta salad, 35
  tuna, bean and sweetcorn salad, 41
turkey:
  Chinese turkey kebabs with 4-minute noodles, 63

v
vegetables, stir-fries, 57
velvet chocolate torte, 102

w
watercress:
  crunchy-topped fish pie, 55
  pea and watercress soup, 23
wraps, 45

y
yoghurt:
  apricot and ginger snap glory, 113
  raspberry cream with crunchy caramelized oats, 110
  strawberry crush, 108
  summer berry brûlée, 110